MORE! Great Games

for 4th-6th Graders

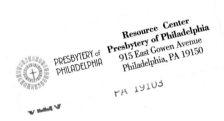

Zondervan/Youth Specialties Books

Adventure Games
Amazing Tension Getters
ArtSource™ Volume 1—Fantastic Activities
ArtSource™ Volume 2—Borders, Symbols, Holidays, & Attention Getters
ArtSource™ Volume 3—Sports
ArtSource™ Volume 4—Phrases & Verses
Attention Grabbers for 4th-6th Graders (Get 'em Growing)
Called to Care
The Complete Student Missions Handbook
Creative Socials & Special Events
Divorce Recovery for Teenagers
Feeding Your Forgotten Soul (Spiritual Growth for Youth Workers)
Get 'Em Talking
Good Clean Fun
Good Clean Fun, Volume 2
Great Games for City Kids
Great Games for 4th-6th Graders (Get 'em Growing)
Great Ideas for Small Youth Groups
Greatest Skits on Earth
Greatest Skits on Earth, Volume 2
Growing Up in America
High School Ministry
High School TalkSheets
Holiday Ideas for Youth Groups (Revised Edition)
Hot Talks
How to Survive Middle School (Get 'em Growing)
Ideas for Social Action
Incredible Stories (Get 'em Growing)
Intensive Care: Helping Teenagers in Crisis
Junior High Game Nights
Junior High Ministry
Junior High TalkSheets
The Ministry of Nurture
More Attention Grabbers for 4th-6th Graders (Get 'em Growing)
More Great Games for 4th-6th Graders (Get 'em Growing)
More Quick & Easy Activities for 4th-6th Graders (Get 'em Growing)
On-Site: 40 On-Location Youth Programs
Option Plays
Organizing Your Youth Ministry
Play It! Great Games for Groups
Quick & Easy Activities for 4th-6th Graders (Get 'em Growing)
Rock Talk
Super Sketches for Youth Ministry
Teaching the Bible Creatively
Teaching the Truth About Sex
Tension Getters
Tension Getters II
Unsung Heroes: How to Recruit and Train Volunteer Youth Workers
Up Close and Personal: How to Build Community in Your Youth Group
Youth Ministry Nuts & Bolts
The Youth Specialties Handbook for Great Camps & Retreats
Youth Specialties Clip Art Book
Youth Specialties Clip Art Book, Volume 2

MORE! Great Games

for 4th–6th Graders

DAVID LYNN

Youth Specialties

Zondervan Publishing House
A Division of HarperCollins Publishers

Disclaimer

Like life, this book contains activities that, in an unfortunate combination of circumstances, could result in emotional or physical harm. Before you use a game, you'll need to evaluate it on its own merit for your group, for its potential risk, for necessary safety precautions and advance preparation, and for possible results. Youth Specialties, Inc., Zondervan Publishing House, and David Lynn are not responsible for, nor have they any control over, the use or misuse of any games published in this book.

More Great Games for 4th-6th Graders

Copyright © 1991 by Youth Specialties, Inc.

Youth Specialties Books, 1224 Greenfield Drive, El Cajon, California 92021, are published by Zondervan Publishing House, 1415 Lake Drive, S.E., Grand Rapids, Michigan 49506

Library of Congress Cataloging-in-Publication Data

Lynn, David, 1954-
    More great games for 4th-6th graders / David Lynn.
      p. cm.—(Get 'em growing)
    Sequel to: Great games for 4th-6th graders. ©1990.
    ISBN 0-310-54171-9
    1. Games—United States. 2. Group games. I. Lynn, David, 1954– Great games for fourth-sixth graders. II. Title. III. Series.
GV1204.12.L964   1991
793'.0973—dc20   91-7302
                                                              CIP

Edited by Sharon Odegaard and Kathi George
Cover Illustration by Dan Pegoda
Designed & Typeset by Leah Perry

Printed in the United States of America

91 92 93 94 95 96 97 98 99 / ML / 10 9 8 7 6 5 4 3 2 1

To the young people and their ministry
at Dove of Peace

Table of Contents

CHAPTER ONE
Play Directions.. 9

CHAPTER TWO
Choosing "It"/Choosing Teams 19

CHAPTER THREE
Touch 'n' Tag Games...23

CHAPTER FOUR
Outrageous Circle Games 29

CHAPTER FIVE
Sure-to-Please Action Games..37

CHAPTER SIX
The Best Races and Relays 45

CHAPTER SEVEN
Fantastic Team Games...53

CHAPTER EIGHT
Wacky Sports Events 1 63

CHAPTER NINE
Wacky Sports Events 2 75

CHAPTER TEN
Slow-Gear Games..83

Acknowledgments

The ideas found in this collection are presented as a compilation of a wide variety of activities suitable for the upper elementary grades. Many of these activities originally appeared in the *Ideas* Library published by Youth Specialties, Inc. The author would like to thank all of the creative people responsible for developing and testing the activities in this book. Without their dedication to young people, this book of great games would not have been possible.

David Lynn

Play Directions

It is during the upper elementary school years that young people develop the skills and abilities that enhance their self-worth and help them make a healthy transition into adolescence and adulthood. Fourth, fifth, and sixth grades—these years lay the groundwork for a child's self-image and identity, affecting the rest of the child's life. Developmental psychologist Eric Erikson long ago discovered that experiences in elementary school gave a child either a sense of competence or feelings of inferiority and helplessness. Children unable to attain a healthy sense of competence develop instead a basic sense of worthlessness, inadequacy, and inferiority, making it more difficult for them to move through the adolescent years successfully.

Before attending school, a child's sense of identity is derived largely from the family. During the elementary school years, however, the influence of the school, church, neighborhood, child care industry, and media all grow significantly. Each of these institutions and people provides children with feedback about who they are. Children evaluate themselves and their competencies by comparing their looks, skills, and abilities with schoolmates, with children they observe on TV and in other media, and with neighborhood kids. As a youth worker, you are concerned about how children feel about themselves because you know how profound an impact self-image has on their lives. Play, believe it or not, has tremendous potential to affect a child's sense of self.

Play gives children the chance to both learn and test out their competencies by showing off new-found motor skills; by exercising their imaginations and sparking their creativity; and by offering them experience in collaborating with peers and adults to achieve a common goal. And all of these can enhance the self-worth of a child.

But play can also have unintended

negative consequences. If young people are placed in situations where only the brightest and the best achieve, what will they learn about themselves? Remember that children evaluate their sense of self and their feelings of worth by comparing their achievements to the achievements of others. Play, whether informal games or formalized sporting events, can easily create in children feelings of insecurity about their competence. Since children do not possess adult coping skills, they have a difficult time separating individual experiences from a general evaluation of their personal worth. They can only handle being picked last for a team so many times before they begin believing that they really are inferior.

Arrange games so that they contribute to every child's sense of competence, rather than creating insecurity. Catering our play experiences to the popular kids, allowing put-downs, or focusing on winning and losing have no place in youth work. Children created in God's image are fragile. We must handle them with care and provide them with play experiences that they can look back upon fondly.

Teaching Kids (and Adults) How to Play

"It's not whether you win or lose, it's how you play the game"—or so we've heard. But somewhere along the way, "how you play the game" was lost. Yet *how* the game is played is why games need to be played. Recapturing this attitude of play is difficult. The following tips can help you restore a playful attitude within your group:

Be patient with children (and adults) who do not know how to have fun play-ing a game. Being "cool" requires a certain aloofness that prohibits some kids from having fun. Others are so preoccupied with winning that they lose the joy of play. Your group may not readily embrace a new philosophy of play. Be willing to give them time and many play experiences in order to lose the cool or jock image.

Young people learn more from watching you than from listening to you. A new attitude toward fun and games will more likely be caught than taught. That means you must start with changing the way adults in your group view games. If your adult leaders sit on the sidelines while expecting the kids to play, then your young people will likely use any excuse to opt out of playing. If your adults push the kids to win, your games will be tense and competitive. If, however, adults who work with children jump into the fun, their excitement will be contagious. When the adults stand along the sidelines, grab their hands and pull them into play. And when they go overboard with competition, gently remind them the purpose of play is not winning, but celebrating by playing.

Competition is not bad; it's the *kind* of competition that you need to monitor. The most appropriate games involve unskilled competition—competition that requires skills that challenge all the players, not just the athletic types. Choose games that require dexterity as well as raw speed, thinking as well as reacting, subjective as well as objective responses. Games that give all the players an equal chance at winning allow everyone to have fun, not just the winners. You know you have healthy competition when the kids forget about keeping score. Structure games to equalize the competition, giving all players an equal chance to participate and succeed. At this age in particular, this is vital!

Choose games for this age group that build self-esteem. Avoid ending a game with a traditional winner (the one on top) and losers (those at the bottom). Structure the winning and losing around team efforts and present the whole team with any awards. Team winning makes it easier for the whole group to feel good about playing. (Be sure the award can be shared by all the team members.) As your kids experience games that teach this new attitude of playing for fun, they will apply it when playing games that are traditionally competitive as well. Even the jock types can learn to want everyone to succeed and to play for the sheer enjoyment of play.

Explain games clearly and quickly. When introducing a game to your group, you first must have everyone's attention. This can be done by extending an invitation for everyone to play. Give people a choice. Then use the following tips to get the game started:

- Assure players, through your gestures and tone of voice, that the game will be fun and will build them up.
- Explain and demonstrate the game in a way that all the players can hear you and see your face. Confusion during the game's explanation will frustrate kids before you even start playing.
- Tell the kids the name of the game, explain step-by-step how to play, and then demonstrate the game with another player or players.
- Show your excitement about playing the game—be a little wild and crazy. If playing the game is fun, why not make

the presentation of the game fun as well? Your play attitude is contagious. Use the KISMIF principle: Keep it simple; make it fun.

- Lead the kids in a practice round of the game. This reassures the group that you want to focus on having fun, rather than on winning and losing. A trial run also builds trust in the play process and in the group.
- Don't take the game so seriously that you get angry with players for not getting the rules. Let your irritation signal you to move on to another game or activity.
- If the game you are explaining requires teams, divide the group before you explain the rules. If the game requires a circle, circle up before presenting the game. This makes it easier to move from the explanation to the demonstration, to the practice round, and finally into the game itself.

Choosing the Right Game

Young people in grades four, five, and six are growing in their skills and abilities. As their speed and endurance increase, they become more accurate in throwing, kicking, dodging, stopping, and starting, and their interest in team competition intensifies. Simply because kids are interested in playing games, however, don't assume that any game will do. Consider the following factors when you select a game from this or any game book.

Decide upon a purpose. Obviously, we lead kids in games so that they can have fun. Although this is important, there are other reasons for playing games as well. Perhaps you want to become better acquainted, burn off energy, practice cooperation, or teach a truth. Playing games can achieve all of these purposes—but you need to know your aim before you can select an appropriate game. Think through what it is you want to accomplish before you choose any activity. And remember, it's okay to play games simply for their enjoyment (Proverbs 17:22).

Include all players. Don't let the "personality trap" dictate your choice of games. Leaders often choose games that the popular, sharp-looking, jock-type kids like. These personality kids then become the litmus test for a game's success or failure. Game leaders who cater to the beautiful kids when selecting games neglect the needs of the other kids that make up a group. Give each of your kids opportunities to be "It," to select a favorite game, or to participate as a Safety Guard. Take a risk and venture into unplayed territory; don't just play the popular favorites.

Involve the players in the choice. Young people, in partnership with adults, need to make play decisions. This does not mean that adult leaders abdicate their responsibilities in favor of kids making all the decisions. Rather, it's young people and adults choosing together the kinds of games they want to play.

Prepare for play. Some games require the leader to prepare game props or to adjust the play area before explaining the game. Some games require the players to come prepared—to wear "grubbies," for example. Choose games for which you and the players are adequately prepared, but don't neglect games that require a little preparation time. The extra work and effort is usually rewarded with great fun.

Be sensitive to the coed question. For some games it's best to separate the boys and the girls. Generally, the more physical the game, the more likely that the girls should play the game separately from the boys. Although boys are not necessarily tougher and girls more fragile, kids in this age group are at different stages of development and won't always be comfortable playing together.

Consider group size. Some games can be played by large groups of young people, while others are more fun with smaller groups of players. Still others can be played equally well with either a small or a large group of players. If you have too many players for a game, break your group into smaller groups or modify how the game is played.

Adjust games for the physically challenged. Mentally retarded, handicapped, and other physically challenged young people need to be included as much as possible in the group's fun. Imagination and prayer can turn up creative ways to involve all kids. If you're playing one of the Wacky Sports Events (see Chapters 8 and 9) that requires kicking a ball, team up the child confined to a wheelchair, for instance, with a child who can run. Allow the child in the wheelchair to throw or bat the ball while the other child runs the pattern. A blind child can be the one that players tag in a relay event. When making modifications to accommodate the physically challenged, however, think safety first!

Go easy on food games. Games and activities requiring the use of food should not be played unless the food is going to be eaten. For example, playing with eggs that will most likely be broken and thrown away gives the wrong message to young people who live in a world where so many people go to bed hungry every night.

You are the final authority. Since you know your kids better than others, it is ultimately up to you to decide which games will be the best for your group. Just because a game is printed in a book does not mean it is suitable or safe *for your group of players*. Please use only the game ideas that best fit your group's personality, locale, size, playing space, and age. Don't be afraid to try something new once in a while, but don't feel you *have* to use a game just because it is in a book.

Choosing Your Play Area

A suitable place for play is as important as the right games. The most important consideration is, of course, safety. Use common sense when selecting a play area. Clear outdoor play areas of rocks, sticks, glass, and other potentially dangerous objects and debris. If the area is suitable except for a little pothole or two, cover them with a Frisbee and point them out to the group. Large holes, protruding sprinkler heads, trees, or other permanent, hazardous objects mean you must find a different play area.

Keep an indoor play area away from windows, stairways, and furniture. Clear the area of dangerous objects or obstacles. Choose only those games that can be safely played in an area the size of yours. Some games designed for large, outdoor spaces just aren't fun if they're played in a confined area.

Safety First
(and Second and Third)

Thinking about safety is a must for every game leader. Common sense will help

you select a game, choose equipment, decide on a place to play, line up adult supervision, and actually play the game. A good rule of thumb: If it doesn't feel safe, assume it's not safe and don't play!

Vitally important to safely playing any game are the *Safety Guards*. A Safety Guard is a "referee plus." Some Safety Guards referee the games, some lead the games, and others participate in play. Safety Guards are given ultimate authority when it comes to running a game. If they see play getting out of hand, they can call a time-out. If a player is participating irresponsibly, a Safety Guard can talk one-on-one with that player about safety. Safety Guards need to be prepared for their role; asking them to read this chapter is a good start.

Although Safety Guards are usually adults, kids can also act as Safety Guards. Designate a different young person as a Safety Guard for each game you play. Rotating the responsibility around the group helps your kids recognize their personal responsibility for safety. Players will take safety more seriously if they have been in the role of Safety Guard.

Ensure the safety of your players and leaders by first playing the game yourself or at least watching as it's played. If you cannot either watch it or play it, get a group of your Safety Guards together and practice the game. This helps you to know what to look for while playing the game with your kids. It's crucial to preview the game to look at as many safety angles as possible. Then, when you teach the kids how to play it, you can include safety precautions with your directions.

The following safety checks can help you and your Safety Guards create a safe and fun playing experience:

- *Boundary check.* Clearly mark boundaries of play and point out the boundaries to the players.
- *Hazards check.* Remove debris and repair or mark other hazards in the playing area. Players need to remove watches, jewelry, pencils, or anything else they are wearing that could hurt them or others during play.
- *Rules check.* State the object of the game and explain its rules step-by-step. Play a practice round to observe if all the players know how to play. Too often players will nod their heads, indicating they understand the rules without really comprehending them. Play more than one practice round if necessary. Players entering the game should first be checked out by a Safety Guard.
- *Break check.* All players should be allowed a personal time-out any time during play. It is imperative that players feel physically and psychologically safe while playing. Players out of breath or feeling threatened by a game need the option to walk away from play. At any time during the game a player can yell, "Break time. Stop!" and play will immediately stop. This offers an immediate out to injured or exhausted players. Explain the time-out and break-time rules before each play event occurs.
- *Safety Guard check.* Are there enough Safety Guards for this game to be safe? Have the Safety Guards been prepared for their roles? These are two questions the game leader must ask herself or himself before play. (By the way, don't play without Safety Guards just because a game in this book does not mention using them.)

Creating Play

Play does not just happen—it is created. Game leaders must create an environment where an attitude of play can flourish.

Consider that players are number one. Players are the reasons you are playing. Don't allow a game to own the players. Empower players with the attitude and skills to own a game. Flexibility is the key. Don't feel locked into strict adherence to a prescribed way of playing a game.

Involve Adults. Young people need to see adults having fun. All too often young people play games with an adult leader while the rest of the adult workers talk to each other on the sidelines.

Plan for the unexpected. Weather, group mood, and attendance are only three of the myriad surprises for a game leader. If you are planning an outdoor event, prepare a few backup indoor games in case of rain, sleet, hail, or gloom of night. As unpredictable as the weather is the mood and interest of your group. What works with your kids one month may not work the next. Plan extra games to spark their interest if things begin to slow down. Be ready for a smaller or larger group than you expected: Either bring a backup set of games for both large and small groups, or be prepared to modify the games you have chosen.

Timing is everything. Let the energy level and fun level of your kids determine how long to play a game. End a game while players are still having fun. If you keep playing until they lose interest, they will remember the boredom rather than the fun of the game. But don't end games so soon that kids feel they didn't have a chance to have fun. Use time to add excitement or lift tension in a game. In some games shortening the time limit hypes kids to play wholeheartedly. If you notice kids looking overwhelmed or frustrated, however, give them more time to play.

There are no such things as official rules. The only rules that should be strictly enforced are the ones that affect safety. Young people in the fourth, fifth, and sixth grades are learning the flexibility and relativity of rules, a skill foundational to more complex learning. Giving children the opportunity to change the rules or create new rules is healthy. At this age one child will say, "Last one to the house is it," and a second child retorts with, "Not included!" The first child then yells back, "No saybacks." This is an example of children using their new-found ability to manipulate rules—all part of normal, healthy development.

Changing the rules or creating new ones is also a great way to energize a game. By modifying rules, players are actually creating a new game. Point out to players that when they change rules and modify games they are taking charge of creating their own play. To keep the playing happy, though, rule changes need to be agreed upon by the group before play begins.

A New Attitude Toward Winning and Losing

Many games have winners and losers, and in most games some players will do better than others. But as a game leader, you can help redefine and refocus the win/lose concept by leading your kids to evaluate their game times, by choosing

team games, by using nontraditional scoring methods, by choosing games that include nonathletic skills, and by making your Safety Guards partners in changing old attitudes of competition.

Take advantage of teachable moments that sometimes follow play events to process what happened during the games. Discuss with the group what they learned from the play experience and how they felt about the competition. Lead them to remember the times during the games when certain players did their best—even if those players did not end up winning. By verbally recognizing nonwinners who either improved or tried their hardest, you help kids learn to enjoy personal stretching rather boasting. (Don't try to evaluate *every* play experience, however.)

Another way to redefine winning and losing is by emphasizing team rather than individual competition. Team winning is different than individual victory because it requires cooperation among the team members to win. And the team that does not win does so as a team, avoiding the focus on one player either winning or not winning. When you discuss with the kids their views on competition, avoid using the word *loser*.

Scoring is another means of refocusing the win/lose concept. Traditional scoring has had the effect of focusing play on the outcome: who wins and who loses. When this is the case with a group of kids, discontinue keeping score. You can create a new challenge and a whole new spirit to game playing by changing the way you score. Begin to give points for things players wouldn't expect. Traditionally points are awarded for the swiftest and the most—but you can give points for the funniest, the most creative, or for cooperation. Doing this also generates new enthusiasm for playing the game, especially when a game begins to slow down. Make sure you include the players when you want to create a new scoring system. Train your players to look for new ways to score the games you play.

Random Scores

Next time your group is having team competition in several events and you want to "neutralize" things so that no team is able to dominate the other teams, here's a way to hand out points that narrows the gap. Before the competition begins, determine the point value for each event. Make sure you have enough points so that every team will receive points following every event. (For example, if you have five teams, you need at least five point entries—10, 8, 6, 4, 2.) Make up a board for each event like the illustration below, and scramble the points so that they are in no particular order.

6	**10**	**2**	**4**	**8**

Then cover the points with construction paper squares with a letter on each one, like so:

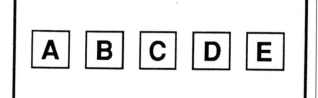

Following every event, the points are awarded this way: The team that comes in first gets *first choice* of the letters on the board. It receives the number of points written underneath the letter chosen. The score is purely chance, but at least it got to choose first. The second place team chooses second, and so on. Sometimes the last place team actually gets the most points because no one knows how many points are behind each letter. The first place team is generally satisfied with the privilege of choosing first, even though in the end the scores are determined by luck. This keeps the competition close and adds extra suspense watching teams choose their letters. Remember, you will need to make up a different board for each event.

Scoring can also be changed by giving away ten points or 100 points to the placing teams or individuals. Kids will want to play their best when they can get 100 or 1,000 points (who wants to play for one point?). Keep the spread between points small so that the last place team or person is still fairly close to the first place. For example, with three teams, first place may be 500 points, second place 475, and third place 450. That way the team in last place still gets lots of points and has achieved something.

Also remember to use unskilled competition when trying to create a new attitude toward winners and losers. If kids know they can compete successfully because different kinds of skills are required, they'll not only be more eager to play but also their idea of who is a winner will change.

Finally, Safety Guards can help you redefine the win/lose attitude. Train your Safety Guards to referee events in such a way that competition is equalized. They can do this by focusing more intently on infractions of the winning teams or individuals and go easier on whoever is behind. The players will soon realize that the Safety Guards are always taking the side of the underdog. After a while players will focus more on having fun rather than earning points or keeping score.

Choosing "It"/ Choosing Teams

This chapter is dedicated to all those adults who have experienced the humiliation of being picked last on a team as a kid. Use these creative games to make a fun and positive game out of a usually tough task.

Adding Up to "It"

Use this game to choose "It" when you've selected a circle game for the group to play. Ask the kids to make a circle. The leader stands in the middle and points to a player while calling out, "Addition." The player then calls out an addition problem, such as "eight plus three." The leader adds the numbers in his head (ask the kids not to make it too hard) and says the answer (in this case, 11—right?). Then, beginning with the player pointed to, the leader counts around the circle. The person receiving the number 11 is "It."

Boxed "It"

All players write their names on slips of paper and place them in a box or sack. Either a leader or a player thoroughly mixes the names while the group watches. Ask someone to draw a name and tell it to the group. The player whose name was drawn is "It."

Boxed Teams

Just as you can choose "It" by putting names in a box and drawing one, so you can choose teams. Place the names of all the players in a box or sack. Mix them around. The leader draws the first two names. These two players are captains on opposing teams, and the two of them rotate turns selecting from the box names to be on each of the teams. It's okay to be chosen last in this fashion because it is random.

Freckle Clumps

As players enter the playing area, all receive a different number of freckles on their faces (put on with a washable felt-tip pen). Mark as many with the same number of freckles as you need members on a team. If you need to break up your group into four teams with ten on a team, for example, ten kids get one freckle, ten kids get two freckles, ten kids get three, and ten kids get four. Once everyone is in and marked, blow the whistle to start the fun. The kids must find out how many freckles they have on their own faces and then locate all the other kids that have the same amount of freckles. When your teams are all divided up, you can play team games or relays.

Get Together

The challenge facing every leader is how to make up teams so that the competition will be relatively even. The old "one-two, one-two" method really doesn't work well for two reasons: first, it doesn't guarantee the same number of boys and girls on each team; second, the kids can rig the teams by quickly getting in line with one person between them and the person they desire to be with. Another problem is that the kids will change teams, and when you get ready to start your first game, 15 are on one team and nine are on the other, and all vow with real gusto that they are on the team to which they were assigned. What's a leader to do? Back up ten yards and punt? No! Outsmart them.

First, ask the boys and girls to form separate lines according to height and hold out their right hands. Mark the back of each hand with washable marking pen. If the kids are switching to stay with friends, change your marking strategy from marking every other person with red to marking two red in a row; then two black in a row. If you prefer not to mark the kids, number them "one, two, three, four, one, two, three, four," and assign the ones and twos to the same team and the threes and fours to the other team. This method will ensure the best possible mix of boys and girls on each team and act as a safeguard against having the teams rigged ahead of time.

Invisible Ink Groups

Here's an easy way to get kids into teams. When they arrive, mark their hands or their necks with invisible fluorescent ink (like the type used at amusement parks to stamp hands for reentry). Don't tell them what mark they receive. You can use a rubber stamp to apply the marks, or use a pen or brush. The ink is available in stationery, art, or novelty shops.

When it's time for the kids to get into groups, turn off the lights and ask them to walk through an ultraviolet light to see which group they're in. You can use an "0" for group one, an "X" for group two, and so on. Kids enjoy the mystery, and the arbitrary marking short-circuits the arguing and changing from one group to the next.

Pinch Me

Here's a wild game that is great for dividing a group into teams. Be sure to advise the players not to be rough. No one is allowed to talk, but laughter and screaming are permitted. Players each receive a slip of paper that they keep

secret from everyone else. On each paper is written one of the following:

    Pinch me
    Poke me
    Tickle me
    Step on my toe
    Scratch my back
    Give me a "high five"

When everyone has a paper, the leader yells, "Go!" and the players must find the others on their team. A "Pinch me," for instance, must go around pinching everyone until he finds someone else who is pinching. These two stick together, pinching others until they find the rest of their team. There should be an equal number in each group. Once teams are assembled, a leader can combine groups to form two or three teams.

Sing-Song Sorting

This game is a great way to divide players into teams. Write ahead of time, on small slips of paper, an equal number of four (or however many teams you want) different song titles that the group knows. As players enter the room or playing area, they receive (at random) one of these song titles. (In other words, if you had 100 kids and you wanted four teams, there would be 25 papers for each of the four different songs.) On a signal, the lights go out and players each start singing the songs they received as loudly as possible. No talking or yelling is allowed, only singing. Players try to locate all the others singing the same song.

Team Tags

This is a great team-choosing game for events where you plan to use name tags or buttons. Color code the name tags or buttons—each color represents a different team. The code can be as simple as drawing a dot or square beside each name with a felt-tip pen. You will then have your group separated into teams in which everyone also knows each other's name.

If the members of your group already know each other well, skip the tags and put a colored dot on every player's hand with a washable felt-tip pen. If you don't want to use different colors to separate teams, draw different geometric figures.

Touch 'n' Tag Games

The toughest thing about tag can be deciding who will begin as "It." Once tag games begin, though, who knows when they will end?

Fizzer Tag

To play this warm-weather outdoor game, drill a small hole in the center of as many Alka-Seltzer tablets as you have players, and then run a string through each tablet to make a loose necklace with one tablet for each player. Ask each player to bring a squirt gun that can be filled in any of several full buckets of water placed out-of-bounds. The object? When a player's Alka-Seltzer tablet absorbs enough dissolving hits to drop off the string, that player is out. To shorten the game, bring out the garden hose!

Glue Tag

In this simple game of tag, the player selected to be "It" is called the "Glue Stick." When "It" yells out, "Glue Stick," all the players scatter. After counting to ten, the Glue Stick begins tagging players as fast as he can. Any player tagged by the Glue Stick must place a hand on the place tagged (Safety Guards can help keep this tasteful with a few well-phrased comments). The second time players are tagged, they must place their other hand over the touched area. With the third tag players are glued to the ground and must freeze in their tracks. The last player to be tagged the third time becomes the new Glue Stick. Play this game in a confined space so the Glue Stick doesn't give up trying to glue all the players to the ground.

Hook-Up

An active game, Hook-Up works best with ten or more people. Divide into pairs, and ask the partners to link elbows. The partner-sets then form a circle. Leave at least four feet between one linked pair and the next linked pair. (In other words, each person in a pair links one elbow with the partner and has the other elbow free.) Then choose one pair to separate and become the "chaser" and the "chasee." The chaser attempts to tag the chasee while both are running inside, outside, and weaving through the circle of pairs. Anytime the chasee wants a break, he can grab the free elbow of one of the pairs. The other member of that pair then becomes the chasee. When the chasee is tagged, she becomes the chaser, and the chaser becomes the chasee.

Human Pinball

The more the merrier in this indoor or outdoor ball-tag game. Give a playground ball to a group of at least ten, then explain the following rules. The object is to be the last one standing after all other players are on their knees.

All players try to send other players to their knees by hitting them below the waist with the ball. Players who are hit with the ball and fail to catch it must kneel. If a player catches a ball, then the player who threw it must kneel. Standing players may chase the ball in order to have a chance to throw it, but they cannot run or walk with it once they grab it—they must throw from where they obtained the ball. Though kneeling players cannot move around, they can still throw the ball at other players while on their knees. If kneeling players hit a standing player with the ball or touch a standing player, they can stand again.

Those players who are touched or hit must kneel. Players can only be hit from the waist down.

Jail Game

The Jail Game is played in and surrounding a good-sized room, preferably one with at least two exits. A jail is constructed in the room by making a square with chairs, tables, or benches. Team A tries to capture all of the members of Team B by tagging them and sending them to jail. Team B, while avoiding being tagged, attempts to free the teammates who are in jail. To free the prisoners players must simply touch the jail. No more than three guards from

Team A can be in the jail room at any time—if there are more than three, all of those in the jail are set free. The round ends when Team A has put all of Team B in jail. At the end of a round or after a designated time period, allow Teams A and B to exchange roles. Team B then tries to put all of Team A in jail. To make it easier, players who have just been freed should have a ten-second count before they can be caught again.

Masking-Tape Maze Tag

If you have a fairly large room with a clean floor, a few rolls of masking tape will set your group up for this fun tag game. This game requires players to pretend that the wide tape strips that you lay down on the floor, maze fashion, represent invisible-though-impenetrable walls that cannot be crossed, jumped, or reached through. You'll want some Safety Guards to watch for corner-cutters and wall-climbers, who can be penalized by being made "It."

An autumn variation can be played outside with lines of raked-up leaves instead of tape.

Popcorn-Blob Tag

Mark off clear boundaries and put spotters on the corners. One person begins

as the "Blob." The Blob then tries to tag or chase one of the other players. If another player is tagged or is chased out-of-bounds, that person becomes part of the Blob. These two join hands and go after a third person who, when tagged, joins hands and helps tag a fourth. The game continues until everyone is part of the Blob. The Blob's only restriction is that it cannot break hands. Thus, only people on the ends can make legal tags. During the course of the game, anyone who steps outside the boundaries becomes part of the Blob. You may need to adjust the size of your playing area if it is too easy or too difficult to catch players.

The catch—and the reason this game includes "popcorn" in its title—is that both the Blob and the players being chased must hop up and down to move. If a player does not hop, he cannot move. Any player caught running, walking, skipping, or anything but hopping becomes a part of the Blob.

For the Blob to be most effective, it must work as a unit. One person should act as the Blob brain and control the Blob by giving directions that other Blob members follow. Tags made when the Blob becomes separated, don't count. Thus, the Blob must go after one person at a time. Once the Blob becomes large enough, it can stretch across the playing field and catch all the remaining players by encircling them.

Safety Tag

A simple game of tag with a twist can be great fun. The twist is having different techniques that a player can use to be safe from being tagged. A player is chosen to be "It." She chases players attempting to tag one of them. Players about to be tagged can do something that keeps them safe—free from being tagged. The following are different types of "Safety Tag."

• Squat Tag—players who squat down are safe and cannot be tagged.
• Nose-and-Knee Tag—players who grab their noses with one hand and their knees with another are safe.
• Hop Tag—players jumping up and down on both feet are safe.
• Dead-Bug Tag—players lying on their backs with their hands in the air are safe.
• Silly-Face Tag—players making silly faces are safe.

Before playing any of the Safety Tag games, warn the kids that a player is safe only for five seconds, then that player is considered fair game for "It" to chase and tag. Modify any of these Safety Tag games to suit your own group's needs.

Sun Tag

For this crazy game of tag you will need an open, outdoor playing space and sunshine. One player is chosen to be "It" and begins chasing all the players, attempting to step on someone's shadow. When "It" succeeds in landing

on a player's shadow, "It" yells, "Sunburn," signifying a successful tag. The tagged player becomes the new "It."

Employ several Safety Guards to make calls on disputed tags.

Squirrel

This game can be played indoors or outdoors. The group forms several small circles of four players each, leaving out two players who become the "squirrel" and the "hound." One person in each circle steps into the middle of the small circle, leaving only three people with hands joined. These three people become a hollow tree, and the extra person becomes a squirrel who finds a home in the hollow tree. The hound chases the extra squirrel in and out between the trees. The squirrel being chased may crawl into any tree for safety, but the squirrel already in the tree must then leave and flee from the hound. If the hound tags a squirrel, that squirrel becomes the hound and the hound the squirrel, and the game continues.

Tire Tag

For a rolling good time, try this form of tag. Obtain an old car tire (not too large). Mark off a playing area that is relatively small compared to the number of players you have. Your group first scatters out on the playing area. "It" then yells out, "Tire Tag," and all players including "It" must freeze in their tracks. "It" rolls the tire at one or more players. Whoever is tagged with the tire becomes the new "It." Players are allowed to jump up and allow the tire to roll through their legs, but if the tire touches them, they are "It." Modify the game by letting your group think of its own versions of tire tag.

Trust Tag

This is the usual game of tag, except it is played with partners. One partner must wear a blindfold while his teammate must guide him by keeping her arms on the blindfolded player's waist (or locking arms) and shouting out directions. The object is for the blindfolded "It" to tag another blindfolded player.

To make it even more difficult, have the seeing player give her partner directions without talking, by just gently pushing or pulling him around.

Underdog

Choose one player to be "It." "It" tags the free players who must freeze when tagged. Frozen players must obtain freedom by spreading their legs apart and allowing a free player to pass between their open legs. "It" must freeze all the free players to end the game. Spice the game up by designating two or three players to be "It."

Outrageous Circle Games

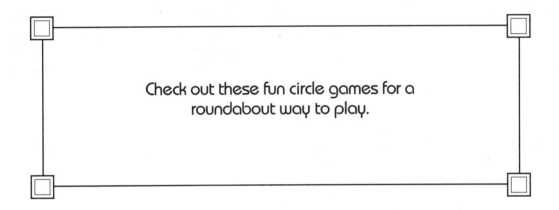

Check out these fun circle games for a roundabout way to play.

Commercial Squirt

Players sit in a circle, and one of them is armed with a loaded squirt gun. The leader asks the player with the squirt gun to identify a well-known product from a clue based on a national TV commercial, a radio jingle, or some local TV or radio commercials. (You could even use questions from a trivia game.) If the player knows the answer, he gets to squirt the people sitting on either side of him once each. If he can't answer correctly, he passes the squirt gun to the person on his right, who then may give the correct answer. If no one guesses the product after three tries, go on to another product. Following are some examples:

Brush your breath with ___ (Dentyne).
Oh, what a feeling, ___ (Toyota).
Those O's will help keep you on your toes: ___ (Cheerios).
Melts in your mouth, not in your hand: ___ (M & M's).
Have you driven a ___ lately? (Ford).
Who said you can't take it with you? ___ (Pepto-Bismol).
Double your pleasure with ___ (Doublemint gum).
How do you spell relief? ___ (Rolaids).

It's a good time for the great taste of _____ (McDonald's).
You work hard, you need _____ (Right Guard).
The choice of a new generation: _____ (Pepsi).

Like a good neighbor, _____ is there. (State Farm).
Trust the _____ touch. (Midas).
The nighttime, sniffling, sneezing, coughing, aching, stuffy head, fever, so-you-can-rest medicine: _____ (NyQuil).

The Contagious Game

Stand or seat kids in a circle so that all can see each other. One person starts the game by describing his "ailment." For example, he might say, "My right eye twitches," so everyone in the group would start twitching his or her right eye. The next person might say, "My left foot has the wiggles," or "I have whooping cough," and everyone must add the corresponding movement to the first movement. After a few people share their ailments, everyone will be jumping, twitching, coughing, sneezing, wiggling, and having a great time. For double laughs, videotape the players to show later. This is also a great game to do with parents and young people as a crowd breaker before an intergenerational activity.

Do What?

You will need a number of small paper strips and balloons. On their paper strips, ask the players to write something silly they would want a group member to do. The instruction should be something that could be done on the spot and it should be in good taste. Remind players that what they write may end up being something they themselves will have to do. All players sign their instruction strips of paper. Some examples of appropriate instructions are as follows:
• Hop around your chair on one leg.
• Bark like a dog for 15 seconds.

• Sing "Mary Had a Little Lamb."
• Take off your shoes.
• Run around the room three times.
• Walk like a crab.

Players are instructed to place their strip of paper in a balloon, blow up the balloon, and tie it. All players should get in a circle with the balloons placed in the center. Select the first "It." A balloon is chosen by the group leader and given to "It," who must sit on the balloon until it pops. "It" then reads the strip of paper and does what it says. The person who wrote the instruction becomes the next "It."

Free-for-All Ball

Once the group is standing in a circle, begin to pass a ball around the circle.

The group must copy the passing technique of the player who begins the pass:

through the legs, behind the back, one hand to the next, over the head. The object is to pass the ball around the circle as quickly as possible. Once the group has caught the rhythm of the passing, start another ball going in the opposite direction. If the group can han-dle this, start a third ball going. The group will have great fun seeing how many balls they can keep going. To make the game live up to its name, yell, "Switch," periodically. When the leader calls out, "Switch," the players must reverse the direction of the ball or balls.

Hanky Snatch

Players can either sit or stand in a circle for this game. If the players are seated, use a large scarf or balloon that takes some time to fall to the ground. If players are standing you can use a handkerchief. Here's how you play. Number players consecutively from one up. The highest number becomes "It." "It" stands in the middle of the circle, yells out someone's number, and drops the hanky, scarf, or balloon. The player whose number was called must catch the object before it touches the ground. If the player fails to catch the object, she is the new "It." If the object is caught, "It" must call another number.

A few helpful hints are in order. If you use balloons, blow up several extras in case any break. Broken balloons count as missed catches. If your group is having difficulty catching the object because it falls too rapidly, ask "It" to throw the object in the air. For added fun have two objects, and have "It" call out two numbers.

Junk Food

This game can involve any number of people. Ask the entire group to sit in a circle with one less chair than there are players. The extra person is "It" and stands in the middle. Everyone is assigned the name of a popular junk food. With large groups you can identify several people with the same junk food name. Generally it is best to avoid having too many different categories so that all the players get a chance to play.

Play begins with "It" calling out the name of one or more junk foods. The people with the names of those junk foods must exchange chairs. During the exchange, "It" tries to claim one of the vacated chairs. The person who fails to get a chair becomes the new "It." The player who is "It" also has the option of calling out, "Junk Food," at which time all players must exchange chairs. Be sure to use sturdy chairs, as this game is really wild—people often end up in each other's laps or on the floor. Safety Guards should be appointed, and they should be ready to intervene when necessary.

King of the Circle

This is a great boys-only game. Mark off a big circle (ten feet or so in diameter) and put about a dozen boys into it. At a signal each boy tries to throw everybody else out of the circle, while trying to stay in the circle himself. The last boy to stay in, wins. You can either play that a body halfway out of the circle is considered out or that if any part of a body touches the circle, that boy is out. You will need several Safety Guards.

Musical Costumes

Here's a funny game that allows everyone to look a little silly. Before you start, fill a laundry bag or pillow case with various articles of clothing—funny hats, baggy pants, gloves, belts, anything that can be worn. (The leader can use discretion as to how embarrassing the items are.) Keep the bag tied shut so the clothing will not spill out.

With the group in a circle, start passing the bag around as music is played. (If you don't use music, use some other random signal like an egg timer or toaster to stop the action.) When the music stops, the person holding the bag must, without looking, remove an article of clothing from the bag, put it on, and wear it for the remainder of the game. Put enough clothes and accessories in the bag so that each person ends up wearing three or four. Use Musical Costumes at seasonal parties—Santa's bag, Easter Parade, instant Halloween costumes. After the game you can have a fashion show or take pictures to hang on a bulletin board.

Name Six

Players sit in a circle. "It" sits in the center of the circle with his eyes closed. The players in the circle pass any object (a ball, a book, a shoe) around the circle until "It" claps his hands, says a letter of the alphabet, and opens his eyes. The player left holding the object must then start the object around the circle again and try to name six objects that begin with the assigned letter before the object gets all the way around again. If unsuccessful, that person becomes the new "It." If the player names all six objects before the ball returns to her, "It" closes his eyes again and the game repeats. (Adjust the number of objects that need to be named to the skill level and size of your group.)

A variation to this game is to have the person caught with the object sing a song before the object gets around the circle again. After clapping his hands, "It" says, "Sing a song," instead of assigning a letter from the alphabet. If it's too easy to sing a song before the object makes it around the circle, simply have "It" count to ten after he claps and says, "Sing a song." The person holding the object must begin singing her song before "It" gets to ten.

Pass It On

With the entire group sitting in a circle, each person is given a safe object of any size or shape to hold. On a signal everyone passes his or her object to the person on the right, keeping the objects moving at all times. When a person drops any object, he must leave the game, but the object remains in play. As the game progresses and more people leave the game, it's harder and harder to avoid dropping an object since there are soon more objects than people.

Ping-Pong Blow

Distribute players evenly around the edge of a large bedsheet so that they can grab its edges and pull it taut (and keep it level). The leader tosses a Ping-Pong ball on the sheet and the players attempt to blow it off. The players between whom the ball drops off the sheet are out, and the circle of players diminishes. (Or, instead of eliminating players, you can play to see how long players can keep the ball on the sheet.) A challenging variation uses a balloon

with a marble inside instead of the Ping-Pong ball. The balloon is less predictable since it isn't a perfect sphere.

Or try using a feather. The kids divide into two teams, one on each side of the sheet, and try to blow the feather away from their side. If the feather touches one of the team members or gets blown over their heads, that team gets a penalty point. The team with the fewest penalty points is the winner.

Scoop

You will need a pie tin, lid, or similar object that can be spun on a floor. Have the group sit or stand in a circle and count off, one number per person. The highest-numbered person begins by spinning the lid on edge in the center of the circle while calling out someone's number. The called person must run to the middle of the circle and pick up the lid before it falls to the ground or stops spinning. If she is successful, she returns to the circle, and the highest-numbered person continues to spin. If the called player is not able to pick up the lid before it stops spinning, she becomes the new "It" and spins the lid while calling out a number.

A challenging variation is for "It" to call out two numbers. The player who grabs the lid first returns to the circle, while the other player becomes the new "It." If neither is successful, the one that was last to leave the circle becomes the new "It." An even more challenging variation suitable for older groups is "Arithmetic Scoop." When numbering the players, begin with 20. "It" then calls out a number using addition, subtraction, or multiplication, depending upon the skill level of your group. If "It" wished to call 21, for example, he would say, "three times seven," or "25 minus four." The players in the circle must do the arithmetic in their heads, and the one whose number was called must quickly run to catch the lid. If you try this variation, use a large platter or garbage can lid that will spin for some time.

Shoot the Duck

This game can be played with any size group from six to 60. Players assemble in one large circle with all the participants facing in the same direction. All place their hands on the shoulders of the person just ahead of them. At various points in the middle of the circle stand players with loaded squirt guns—about one shooting player for every three players in the circle.

At a given signal (or when the music starts) the players in the circle walk around the shooters in the middle. When the music stops, the shooters fire one shot at the players (the "sitting ducks") immediately in front of them. The ones who have been shot must leave the game. The circle then closes up and the music begins again. The circle again moves around until the music stops and the ducks are shot. This procedure continues until only one duck is left, and she is declared the winner. (As more and more players leave the game the leader might want to decrease the number of shooters.) This game is exciting and the tension runs high.

Sponge Dodge

In the heat of the summer, find a beach or open lawn, take along several five-gallon buckets, an equal number of sponges, and cool yourselves off with this game. Mark out a circle and place the buckets around the perimeter. Fill them halfway with water, and drop a sponge in each. After all the players get in the middle of the circle, the leader soaks the first sponge and throws it from her position outside the marked circle. Those who get hit join the leader around the edge to throw sponges at the players in the middle. The game continues until only one player is left. Sponges that drop inside the circle can be retrieved by any thrower, but they must be dipped again before they are thrown. Some variations:
- Reverse the game. That is, when the thrower hits someone, the thrower joins those inside the circle.
- Play by teams. Time how long it takes for one team to get all members of an opposing team hit and out of the cir-

cle. Shortest time wins. Or set a time limit: the winning team has the most members still in the circle when the clock runs out.
- Run the game indefinitely with no winners or losers. Begin the game with five inside the circle. Whoever makes a hit trades places with the victim.

States

Everyone sits in a circle and takes the name of a state (Tennessee, Oregon, and so on). Every person should choose a different state, and the chosen states are named out loud. One person chosen to be "It" begins the game by standing in the middle of the circle with a soft, rolled-up newspaper. When the news-paper-wielding "It" calls out the name of a state, the person who represents that state must stand up and call out the name of another state before "It" can whack him below the knees with the newspaper. The round continues until "It" whacks a player before the player calls out another state. The whacked player becomes the new "It."

A few guidelines are as follows: You must call the name of a state that is represented in the group. If a player in the circle goofs and calls a state not found in the group, that player becomes "It." A player cannot call the state that just called him. If a player does so, he becomes "It."

Action can get fast and furious between just a few states, so occasionally redistribute the states among the players to give everyone a chance to participate.

Trick Ball

Players sit in a circle facing inward with their arms folded. "It" sits in the middle holding a foam ball or sponge. "It" has two options: throw the ball to someone sitting in the circle, or fake a throw to someone. If a person unfolds her arms to catch the ball or sponge when "It" fakes a throw or if a person fails to catch a real throw, that person becomes the new "It," and the two switch places. If a person is not faked out or does catch a thrown ball, then "It" must try again with a new player.

Sure-to-Please Action Games

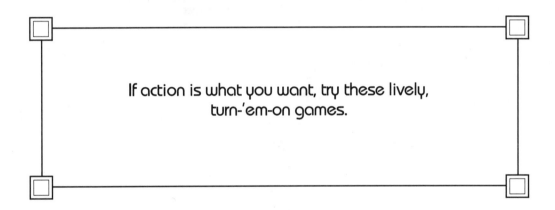

If action is what you want, try these lively, turn-'em-on games.

Blind Balloon Hunt

Begin by placing a number of balloons in random locations on a large floor or field (if on a field, they may need to be anchored). The players are divided into groups of three kids each. One player on each team is selected to be the hunter. The other two players from each team are the guides. Blindfold each of the hunters. At the whistle or other signal, the hunters attempt to locate as many balloons as possible with the help of the guides, and bring them back unbroken to a starting point. (All groups of players hunt at the same time.) The guides may not touch the hunter or the balloons and can only give verbal commands to lead the hunters to the balloons. Allow as much time as you feel is necessary. The team with the most balloons when time is called wins. Announce the time remaining every so often to add excitement to the hunt.

Carry-'n'-Crumple

Play this wild and crazy newspaper game anytime and almost anywhere. All you need to play is a stack of newspapers and a safe playing area marked into zones (see diagram below). You may use chairs or tape to create each team's zoned area. Divide the group into two or more teams of four to eight players per team. Assign a Safety Guard to each team. Team members huddle in their zoned playing areas. There should be a stack of newspapers behind each of the zones. Decide ahead of time how many pieces of newspaper to give each team; there should be an equal number of individual pieces of newspaper per team. On the word "Go!" all players rush to their stack of newspapers. Each player is allowed to grab only one individual piece of newspaper. As soon as a

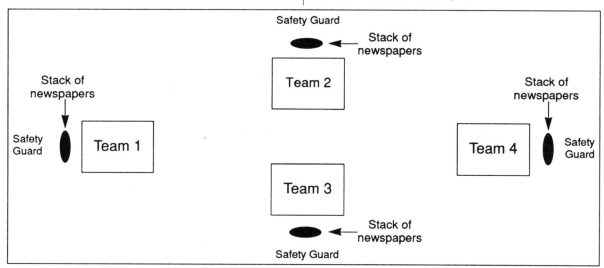

player has his or her piece of newspaper, he or she can run back to the zoned playing area, sit down on the ground or floor, and crumple up the newspaper *using only one hand*. Once the newspaper is tightly crumpled, to the satisfaction of the Safety Guard, the player can go back to the stack of newspapers, grab another individual piece, run back to the zoned playing area, sit down, and crumple up the new piece— again to the satisfaction of the Safety Guard. This process is repeated by each team's players until the entire stack of newspapers is crumpled into a pile. Once a team has completely crumpled its stack of papers, team members can begin firing their wads of paper into the zones of the other team or teams. A team does not have to wait for other teams to complete crumpling before they can begin firing. A team must finish crumpling its entire stack of newspapers before its Safety Guard allows players to fire on other teams. The object of the game is to throw as many wads of newspaper as possible into the zones of the other teams within a specified period of time. To count, a wad must fall within another team's zoned area. Players can bat away incoming newspaper wads, but once a wad lands it cannot be thrown out of the zoned area. The team with the fewest wads of crumpled newspaper in its zoned playing area wins at the end of the time period.

Clothespin Challenge

Two players sit in chairs facing each other with their knees touching. Each is shown a large pile of clothespins at the right of their chairs. Each is then blindfolded and given two minutes to pin as many clothespins as possible on the pant legs of the other player. If you have a small group and enough clothespins and blindfolds, line all the players up facing each other. Rotate players after each round until each of the players has had an opportunity to face off with several other players.

Clothes Pinning

Here's a wild game that is simple yet fun to play with any size group. Give everyone in the group six clothespins. On "Go!" each player tries to pin his or her clothespins on other players' clothing. Each of a player's six pins must be hung on six different players. Players need to keep moving to avoid having clothespins

hung on them. When players have no clothespins left, they remain in the game, attempting to avoid being pinned. When the leader blows a whistle, play stops and the group takes time to recover before playing another round.

A variation of this game is to reverse it. Players hang their six clothespins on themselves in visible locations like on a shirt or pants. The object is for a player to get other players' clothespins and hang them on himself.

Flyswatter

Instead of playing "Pin the Tail on the Donkey," try this crazy variation. Blind- fold a player, give him a flyswatter (the type with holes in it), and spin him around a few times. Place a glob of shaving cream on the wall, and have the player try to swat it. The other players can coach the blindfolded player, but they may not touch him. It can get a little messy, so don't play this game unless you are prepared to do some cleaning up. Give each player a chance. Wipe up shaving cream after each attempt and put it in a different spot for the next player.

Hunters and Hounds

Players pair off, one being the "hunter" and the other being the "hound." The hunters each get a small box or sack, and the hounds try to go out and find (for the hunters) peanuts that have been hidden beforehand around the room. When a hound finds a peanut, he cannot touch it, but begins to howl, and his corresponding hunter comes and retrieves the peanut. When two or more hounds find the same peanut, each howls, and the hunter who gets there first gets the nut. All hunters wait in a "lodge" (a circle or specified area) until their hounds howl. Hunters must return to the lodge after retrieving a peanut. If a hunter's hound begins howling before that hunter has reached the lodge, that hunter must return to the lodge before leaving to retrieve the peanut the hound has found.

Kubic Kids

For this simple, fun game, draw a square on the floor (using chalk or masking tape) and see how many kids and adult leaders can get inside the square. Anything is legal, as long as no one is hurt and no part of the body is touching the floor outside the square. Keep time and play several rounds of the game so the group can compete against the best time.

Marshmallow Pitch

Group the players in threes and give each a sack of miniature marshmallows. One person in each threesome begins by being a "counter," one is a "pitcher," and one is a "catcher." On "Go!" the pitcher tosses a marshmallow to the catcher, who is standing about ten feet away. The counter counts how many successful catches are made. After 20 throws the three trade places, and the pitching, catching, and counting resume for another 20 throws. The three trade places one more time so that all three players have an opportunity to count, pitch, and catch. Safety Guards tally the total number of marshmallows caught by each team.

Nickname Ball

Allow time for all the players to nickname themselves (not using put-downs). You will need a wall on which a playground ball can be bounced safely. One player is chosen to be "It" to begin play. "It" bounces the ball in such a way that it bounces off the floor or ground before bouncing off the wall. At the same time "It" calls out the nickname of another player. The player whose nickname is called must catch the rebounding ball before it hits the floor or ground again. If the nicknamed player is able to catch the ball, "It" continues to bounce the ball off the wall until a nicknamed player misses it. Any player not catching a rebounding ball becomes the new "It."

Shooting Gallery

Blindfold several adult leaders and give them kazoos or party noisemakers. They are the "ducks" in this shooting gallery, moving back and forth and bobbing up and down behind a wall or board that's about five feet high, making duck noises all the while. From about ten feet away, kids have five throws of a beach ball at the ducks. No need to keep score. It's fun just to see how often you can score a hit.

Tin Pan Bang Bang

The leader stands on a chair in the middle of the room with a stainless steel pot in her hand and a metal spoon. The crowd begins milling around the room. Everybody has to keep moving. The leader then bangs on the pot with the spoon a certain number of times. The players count the number of beats and then hold hands in a circle containing the same number of persons as the number of beats. Those who are not in a circle with the right number of people when a whistle blows are eliminated from the game. This is continued, with a varied number of beats each time, until all are eliminated except for one person. That person becomes the new leader for the next round of play.

Up Balloon

This is a fun variation of musical chairs that uses balloons instead of chairs and no music. Everybody should blow up a balloon. One balloon should be taken out of the group (two, if the group is large). The group members should huddle together with their balloons. On the command, "Up Balloon," all group members throw their balloons up in the air. Then players try to catch a balloon. Since you have taken out one or two of the balloons, one or two of your group members will end up without a balloon. Whoever is without a balloon is out of the game. Do not replace popped balloons. If a balloon pops in the air, there is one less balloon. Or if a balloon pops while a player is holding it, that player is eliminated. Play continues until only one player is left.

Water Balloon Catapult

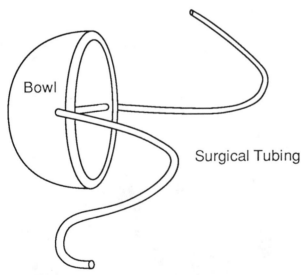

Bowl

Surgical Tubing

This has to be one of the most exciting and fun game ideas you will ever use.

Punch two holes in a plastic bowl near the rim and slide a long piece of surgical tubing through the holes. Tie the ends of the surgical tubing to two stakes or poles. Place water balloons in the bowl, pull back the tubing, and let 'em fly. You should be able to lob balloons up to 40 yards without any trouble. Of course, you can have two teams face each other in battle or try to lob the balloons directly at certain targets. **Caution:** This can be dangerous and destructive. If balloons are lobbed low or at close range, they can dent a car or break windows or hurt someone. Keep your Safety Guards posted and ready to intervene, if necessary.

Whirling High Jump

Get three volunteers to come forward and try this simple game. Give each a stick about 18 inches long. Tell each person to hold the stick straight out at arm's length with both hands so that he or she can watch it while turning around 50 times. The volunteers then must drop the stick and jump over it. Whoever jumps the farthest is the winner. Of course, most kids get so dizzy they can't even *see* the stick when they drop it, let alone jump over it. It's fun to watch. Have the rest of the group count as the volunteers turn around. **Safety note:** Remove all chairs and other obstacles that might be in the way of the jumpers. Keep your Safety Guards on the alert for any possible safety problems.

The Best Races and Relays

Looking for a game to get your group on the move?
These may be just the games you need. There is nothing
like a great relay or race to get kids excited!

Back-Up Relay

Have two people (same sex) race to a point, face each other, and hold their arms straight up in the air. Someone from their team places a ball between them. They must simultaneously make a 360-degree turn without the ball falling to the ground. They return to their team and the next two people do the same. If the ball falls, they must start over.

Balloon-Bat Relay

Divide your kids into two teams, and have them line up single file with the players as close together as possible. Players should straddle their legs and leave enough space between one player and the next so that they can "bat" a balloon down the line through their legs with their hands. This is not easy if all the players are standing close together. The person at the front of the line starts the balloon back. When the balloon reaches the last person in the line, that player takes it to the front and starts the balloon back through the line. This continues until the team is once again in starting order.

Big-Mouth Stack

Here's a great race game. The object of the game is to see how high teams can stack regular alphabet blocks. The catch is that players cannot use anything except their mouths to place the blocks on top of each other. (Remember to wash the blocks after every use.)

Bucket Brigade

Each team lines up single file with a bucket of water at the front of the line and an empty bucket at the back of the line. Each team member has a paper cup. The object of the game is to transfer the water from one bucket to the other by pouring the water from cup to cup down the line.

You may have two winners: the first team to empty the full bucket, and the team whose empty bucket ends up with the most water.

Centipede Race

Here's a great game that can be played indoors or out. All you need are some benches. Seat as many players as possible on each bench, with them straddling it like a horse. When the race starts, everyone must stand up, bend over, and pick up the bench, and hold it between their legs. They then move like a centipede to a finish line 40 or 50 feet away. It's a lot of fun to watch.

Clothespin Relay

String a clothesline from one end of the room to the other, shoulder high to the average person. Place as many clothespins as you have team members on the line. Teams line up facing the clothesline. The object is to run to the line, remove one clothespin with one's teeth (no hands), and bring it back to the team. All team members do the same in relay fashion. The first team to retrieve all its clothespins wins.

Cyclops

For this game, the group is divided up into teams of three to five, and a volunteer is selected from each team. Each team is given a box of materials, including tape, newspaper, aluminum foil, and similar items. On the word, "Go!" the team (henceforth called the "pit crew") uses the materials to cover the volunteer completely, except for one eye.

Once the volunteer is completely covered, a Safety Guard checks the "cyclops" out. If no clothing or skin is showing, the cyclops may attack (tag) any other cyclops who is not yet completely covered. The pit crews may not interfere with or assist in the attack. No cyclops may attack without permission from a Safety Guard. Once an unprepared cyclops is tagged, he is eliminated. The unprepared cyclops may flee the tag, however, and the pit crew may keep working on the cyclops while he is fleeing. The attacking cyclops may remain in pursuit until a piece of her covering falls off and some skin or clothing shows through. If this should occur, the attacking cyclops must stop and allow her pit crew to make the necessary repairs. The event continues until there is only one cyclops left.

Doughnut-Tongue Shuffle

After dividing the group into two equal teams, ask the teams to line up single file. Give the first person in each line a large doughnut (preferably plain). On a signal, the first person in each group must run up to and around a given obstacle while holding the doughnut by sticking his tongue through its hole; no hands allowed. (This usually requires that the head be tilted back and the tongue pointed upward.) After running around the obstacle, the runners go to a designated area where a judge is waiting. Then each runner must eat his doughnut. The doughnut must be completely eaten (to the satisfaction of the judge) before the runner receives another doughnut from the judge. The runner then carries this second doughnut to the next person in the relay line. The first runner places the doughnut in position on the next runner's tongue, and the relay continues. The first team to complete the relay by running all of its members shouts, "The Doughnut-Tongue Shuffle!" and wins.

Driving the Pigs to Market

The teams are lined up behind the starting line. Give the first player a "wand" (a yardstick or broom handle) and a "pig" (a plastic soda bottle). At the signal, the first player drives the pig to the goal and back by pushing it with the wand. The second player does the same until all have driven a pig to market. The first team to complete the cycle wins.

Fan the Balloon

Each team gets a balloon and a fan (which can be anything—an old record album cover, a newspaper, or a magazine). On the signal, each player on the team must fan the balloon around a goal and back. The players cannot touch the balloon, and the balloon cannot touch the floor.

Happy Handful Relay

This relay can be easily adapted for indoor or outdoor use. Assemble two identical sets of at least 12 miscellaneous items (two brooms, two balls, two skillets, two rolls of bathroom tissue, two ladders). Use your imagination to collect an interesting variety of identical pairs of objects. Place the two sets of objects on two separate tables.

Choose a team for each table. The first player for each team runs to her table, picks up one item of her choice, runs back to her team, and passes the item to the second player. The second player carries the first item back to the table, picks up another item, and carries both items back to the third player. Each succeeding player carries back to the table the items collected by his teammates, picks up one new item, and carries them all back to the next player. The game will begin rapidly, but the pace slows as each player decides which item to add to a growing armload of items. It also takes more and more time for one player to pass his burden to the next player in line.

Once picked up, an item cannot touch the table or floor. Any item that is dropped in transit or transfer must be returned to the table by the leader. No one may assist the giving and receiving players in the exchange of items except through coaching. The first team to empty its table wins.

Iceberg Relay

This is a great idea for a swimming party. Players push or pull a block of ice to the opposite end of a swimming pool and back. It's frigid. Use several blocks of ice and award prizes for the best time.

Inner Tube Relay

Each team breaks into either same-sex or mixed pairs and lines up at different starting points around the room. Inner tubes (one for each team) are placed in the center of the room. Each pair of team members must run to the inner tube and squeeze through the tube together, starting the tube over their heads and working it down. The first team whose pairs finish wins. Inner tubes should be regular auto size (not too small or large).

Inner Tube Roll Relay

This challenging game can be played indoors or out-of-doors. Divide the group into teams with an even number of people on each team. Then each team has its members pair up. The first couple from each team stands behind the starting line. A large, inflated inner tube is placed on the floor between them. At the sound of the whistle, the couple must stand the tube up and together roll it around a chair and back to the starting line without using any hands. If the inner tube falls while a pair is rolling it, the pair must come back to the starting line and begin again. The pairs are not allowed to kick the inner tube along while lying down. When a couple successfully completes the round trip, the next pair of teammates places the tube flat on the floor, and without using their hands, they stand it up and "keep on tubin'." The first team to have all of its couples successfully complete the relay is the winner. If teams do not have even numbers, use the extra player as the Referee.

Let It Blow

Divide your group into teams, and give each person a deflated balloon. On a signal, the first person on each team blows up her balloon and lets it go to sail through the air. That person must then go to where the balloon lands, blow it up again, and let it go. The object is to get the balloon across a goal line 15 to 25 feet away. When a player's balloon crosses the goal, she runs back to tag the next player on the team, who must do the same thing. This game is really wild, since it is almost impossible to predict where the balloons will land each time. It is especially fun when played outside, because the slightest breeze blows the balloon in a different direction. (Keep some extra balloons on hand.)

Long Jump Relay

Divide the group into teams of six to eight players, mark a starting line, and have the team members stand behind the line in single file. At the signal, the first player on each team takes a standing broad jump straight ahead (both feet must leave the ground simultaneously). The next player in line then runs up to the first player who moves aside so the second player can place his feet exactly where the first player's feet were. The second player then does another standing broad jump. The third player runs up to the second and repeats the process. Each player in turn rushes forward and jumps from where the preceding player landed. After the last player of every team has jumped, the total distance of each team is measured. The farthest distance wins.

News Relay

Teams line up on one end of the room. On the other end, hang the front page of a newspaper, several clippings, or a whole newspaper. (You can also use the newspaper comics or your Sunday school quarterly.) Prepare questions on the news stories ahead of time. You ask a question, and one person from each team runs to the newspaper and locates the correct answer. The first to shout it out wins.

Plop-Plop-Fizz-Fizz Relay

Provide enough Alka-Seltzer tablets for each player. Fill several pitchers of water (enough to fill the cupped hands of team members) and bring towels for cleaning up. Line teams up in relay style. At the signal, send the first kid in each line down to the pitchers to grab one, return, and begin pouring water into the cupped hands of each team member. Meanwhile, the person immediately behind each recipient of the water places an Alka-Seltzer tablet into the makeshift "cup" in front of him. The first team to *completely* dissolve all of its Alka-Seltzer tablets is the winner.

Sack Race

Obtain a number of burlap bags (potato sacks) or pillowcases and divide the group into teams. The teams line up, and the first player in each line gets into the sack, feet first, and holds the sack up while hopping around a goal and back. On completion, the next player gets the sack and does the same thing. If you decide to use old pillowcases, players must hop more slowly so they don't rip the pillowcases.

Sock Race

Seat two teams in two circles within reach of a huge pile of worn out (but clean) socks. On the signal, each player tries to put as many socks on her feet as possible in the time allowed (usually two minutes).

Surprise Bag Relay

Teams line up single file behind a line. A paper bag containing individually-wrapped, edible items is placed on a chair, one chair per team, some distance from the teams' starting lines. On a signal, the first player in each line runs to her team's chair, sits down, reaches into the bag without looking, pulls out an item, unwraps it, and eats it. When she has swallowed the entire contents of the package to the satisfaction of the Safety Guard, she runs back to the starting position and tags the next player who then takes his turn. Each player must eat whatever is grabbed out of the bag. Suggestions for the surprise bag include

a small green onion
a can of warm soda
a raw carrot
a piece of cream cheese
a candy bar
a half of a peanut butter sandwich
an orange
a handful of peanuts
a stalk of celery

There should be nothing that could make the players sick.

Toilet Paper Race

Teams race to see who can unroll and then roll back up a roll of toilet paper by pushing it along with their noses. Players take turns unrolling—each player unrolling for ten seconds before switching. When all the players have had a turn, the first player goes again, and so on, until the toilet paper has been unrolled and rolled up again. The toilet paper can be rolled anywhere within a defined playing area. When the roll is undone, a Safety Guard can help a player start to reroll it since this is difficult to accomplish with one's nose.

Typhoon

Here is an ideal summertime game. Line up two teams single file, facing a water source. At a signal, the first player in each line runs to the water, fills a soft plastic bucket, returns to his team, and throws the water in the face of the next-in-line teammate. Before the player can throw the water, his teammate must point and yell, "Typhoon!" Each person takes the bucket down to the water and returns to storm his team. The first line to finish is declared the winner.

For safety reasons, the players throwing water should be at least three feet from those getting doused, and a plastic bucket must be used. Post Safety Guards at each line. You'll be surprised how many times the group will want to play this game on a hot day.

Fantastic
Team Games

Children at this age love team competition. Stir in a healthy dose of unskilled competition, add a dash of cooperation, and watch them have fun!

Balloon Extermination

After dividing the group into two teams, give each team the opportunity to name itself. Allow the teams to mingle in a defined play area. One of the Safety Guards at any point during the mingling throws a balloon into the air. Team A tries to keep the balloon in the air and away from the destructive forces of Team B, which attempts to break the balloon as fast as it can. Once the balloon is broken, the two teams switch roles. Keep time to see which team can break the balloon the fastest. Average the times to see which team took the shortest amount of time to exterminate the balloons. You will need to have a number of balloons available. If you play outside, encourage the players to wear sunglasses to protect their eyes from popping balloons.

Berserk

Here is a unique game that requires little skill, includes any amount of people, and is 100 percent active. The object is for a group of any size to keep an equal amount of assigned tennis balls moving around a gymnasium floor until six penalties have been incurred.

The vocabulary for this game is unique and essential to the success of the game. It goes like this:

Rabid Nugget: a moving tennis ball.

Hectic: a stationary tennis ball.

Berserk: a Safety Guard's scream, designating a penalty or safety violation.

Frenzy: an elapsed time period measuring six *Berserks.*

Logic: a tennis ball that becomes lodged unintentionally on or behind something.

Illogic: a tennis ball that is craftily stuck on or behind something (in an attempt to decrease the number of *Rabid Nuggets* the players must keep in motion).

Paranoia: a player's feeling that the Safety Guards are picking on him.

If 30 players are on the gym floor, 30 *Rabid Nuggets* are thrown, rolled, or bounced simultaneously onto the floor by the Safety Guards. There need to be at least three Safety Guards: one at each end of the court and one off the side at mid-court. A number of wandering Safety Guards are also recommended. It is the duty of the two Safety Guards on the floor to try to spot *Hectics* and to generate a hysterical scream (a *Berserk*) so that all will recognize a penalty. The players have five seconds to start a *Hec-*

tic moving again or another full-throated *Berserk* is issued. The Berserking Safety Guard must point condemningly at the *Hectic* until it is again provided impetus.

Every 15 seconds after a start, the sideline Safety Guard puts an additional *Rabid Nugget* into play until the final *Berserk* has been recorded.

The team is allowed six *Berserks,* at which juncture the Safety Guard on the sideline (who is responsible for timing this melee), jumps up and down waving her arms and yelling, "Stop! Stop! Stop!"

The object is to keep the *Rabid Nuggets* moving as long as possible before six *Berserks* have been recorded. This time span is called a *Frenzy.* After a *Frenzy,* ask the group to develop a strategy in order to keep the *Rabid Nuggets* moving for a longer span of time, in other words, increasing the *Frenzy.*

Other rules are as follows:

1. A *Rabid Nugget* may only be kicked randomly or to another player. It may not be held underfoot and simply moved back and forth.

2. If a *Rabid Nugget* becomes a *Logic,* the Safety Guard must get the *Nugget* back into motion.

3. Official tennis balls are not essential to active and satisfying play. You could probably have a great game if all the players brought their own piece of Silly Putty.

David and Goliath Sling Throw

Divide the group into two teams ("David One" and "David Two") with the same number of boys and girls on each team. Each team is given one old nylon stocking and one whiffle ball to place inside the toe of the stocking. One person of

the same sex from each team steps forward to the throwing line. They twirl the stockings over their heads or at their sides and then see who can throw the stockings the farthest. Each winner gets ten points. The team with the most

points wins the contest.

You can then repeat this contest for accuracy. Set a "Goliath" (a chair or other object) approximately 20 to 30 feet from the throwing line. The person who comes closest gets 20 points for his team. If the thrower should hit "Goliath," an additional ten bonus points are awarded. The kids will quickly find out that it took much practice for David to be such a skilled marksman.

Caution: Be sure that the teams are 20 yards or more to the sides of the throwing line because the slings can go forward, backward, or straight up when the kids throw them.

Desperation

Two teams get on opposite sides of the room, staying behind a line. For each round, one person from each team is blindfolded. A squirt gun is then placed between the two teams. On "Go!" the two blindfolded players try to find the squirt gun. Their teammates may help them by yelling out directions. As soon as one of the players finds the squirt gun, he removes his blindfold and squirts the other player, who is still blindfolded. The player who does not find the squirt gun may try to run back behind her team's line to avoid being squirted, but she may not remove her blindfold. It is illegal to remove the blindfold before the squirt gun is found or while a player is being pursued by the one with the squirt gun.

Points are scored as follows:

	Points
Finding the squirt gun	50
Squirting the other player	50
Removing the blindfold illegally	minus 100

This game can also be played outdoors on a warm day using water balloons.

Giant Scrabble

For this game you will need to make two sets of large cards, each one with a letter of the alphabet printed on it. Make several extra vowels (A, E, I, O, U) for each set. Two teams form a huddle on either side of a room. Place the stacks of cards in the middle of the room. A leader calls out a classification, such as football teams, ice cream flavors, or clothes. The two huddled teams decide on a word from the called-out classification, like "the Rams," "chocolate chip," or "jeans." After choosing a word, both teams run to the pile of letters, select the ones that spell their word(s), rush back to their team spots, and line up to spell the word(s). Each team member holds one letter. The team with the longest word receives two points. The team with the fastest time receives one point. (Or you can create your own point system.)

Grape Toss

Teams appoint one player to be the "tosser." She gets a bag of grapes. The rest of the team forms a circle around the tosser, who must toss grapes, one at a time, to everyone on her team. Each team member must catch the grape in his mouth before the tosser can toss to the next player. The first team to go around its circle successfully wins. Wash the grapes before giving them to the teams, and ask the tossers to wash their hands before tossing. Remind the team players to watch out for choking while swallowing their grapes.

Ice Melting Contest

Each team is given a 25-pound block of ice. Each ice block is weighed in, and the teams are given ten minutes to melt as much of it as possible. No water, fire, crushing, or chipping of the ice is allowed. At the end of ten minutes, each block is weighed again. The block that lost the most weight wins.

Letter Flash

All you need for this flashy game is a set of alphabet cards. These can easily be made by printing the alphabet on 8½" x 11" paper, one letter per page. The print should be large, capital letters. Break the group into two or more teams and you are ready to play. The members of each team should sit closely together.

The game leader, who is not on a team, holds up one of the letters of the alphabet so that all the team members can easily see it. When the leader flashes a letter, he also yells out a category. Categories can be any general topic with which the teams are familiar. Some possible categories are cereal brands, cartoons, shoe brands, school subjects, Bible stories, types of cars, or video game titles. The first player to respond with the name of a specific item from the called category that begins with the flashed letter wins the letter for her team. For example, if the letter were C and the category Bible stories, a player yelling out "Cain and Abel" before any other responses would win the letter C for her team. The letter is given to the winning team and cannot be used again during that round of play. The game leader judges whether or not an answer is valid. The team with the most letters at the end of a specified playing time wins. It works well to set a time limit for the response after a letter is flashed. If no team responds correctly during the specified time period, the letter is set aside and cannot be used again until another round of play.

Match Up

Divide into two or more teams of equal number. Have each team choose a team captain who goes to the front of the room with the other team captain(s). Everyone, including the team captains, should have several sheets of paper and pencils.

The leader then asks the entire group a question, such as, "What is your favorite holiday?" Everyone, without any discussion, writes down his or her answer on one slip of paper and passes it to the team captain, who has also written down an answer. No talking is allowed during this time. When ready, the team captains announce their answers, and ten points are awarded to each team for every answer from that team that matches their team captain's. In other words, if the team captain answered "Christmas," then the team would get ten points for every other answer of "Christmas" from that team.

The following are some sample questions:

1. If you were going to repaint this room, what color would you paint it?
2. What country in the world would you most like to visit?
3. What is your favorite subject in school?
4. What book of the New Testament do you like the most?
5. What is your favorite TV show?
6. Choose a number between one and five.
7. What is your favorite Bible story?

Plunder

Divide the group into two teams that line up on opposite sides of the room. In the middle of the room pile several safe items that you have collected (books, coats, shoes, balls, shoe-strings, church bulletins, chalkboard erasers). At the signal, all the players from both groups run to the pile and grab one item at a time to carry back to their team's collection box. As soon as players deposit their items, they may return to pick up one more item each until the pile is gone.

Position a Safety Guard at each team's container. Infractions can be penalized by asking a player to wait 15 seconds before returning to the middle for another item. Whoever grabs an item first gets the item. If two players from opposing teams both grab an item at the same time, a Safety Guard flips a coin to determine which player gets the item. Have several Safety Guards available near the pile.

When all the items have been removed from the center of the room, count the items each team has collected. The team with the most items wins. Play as many rounds as you like.

The Point Game

Give everyone a score card similar to the one below. Read each item aloud and have the kids score themselves. You can also play by teams. Players keep track of their points as specified. The person with the most points wins. Make up your own scorecard with 20 items, such as the following:

1. Ten points if you are wearing red. _____ points.
2. Ten points for every penny in your pocket. _____ points.
3. Ten points if you have a white comb. _____ points.
4. Your shoe size equals the number of points you receive. Half sizes get next highest points. _____ points.
5. Fifteen points if your birthday is on a holiday. _____ points.
6. Ten points if you have ever ridden a train. _____ points.
7. Ten points if you have a pen with you. _____ points.
8. Ten points if you are wearing white socks. _____ points.
9. Ten points if you brought your Bible. _____ points.

Total _____ Points

Posture Perfect

Two teams line up facing each other. One player from each team stands between the lines. Both demonstrate any four postures—standing on tiptoe, thumbs in ears, ballerina—while the other players watch closely. A Safety

Guard writes down each of the four demonstrated postures on separate slips of paper.

One of the players in the middle selects one of the slips of paper, silently reads the description of the posture, and calls out, "Posture Perfect." All players on both teams assume one of the four postures as fast as possible. The object of the game is for players to assume one of three postures *not* written on the selected paper. When all players have assumed a posture, the caller reveals the posture described on the slip of paper she holds. Any player on either team who has assumed this posture must go to the "posture perfect prison," a designated area away from the two teams.

The caller returns the slip of paper to the Safety Guard, the other player in the middle chooses a slip of paper, and the game repeats. (The two players in the middle of the lines alternate choosing.) The team with the most players left in line after a designated time period wins the game.

Skizbomania

Here's a search-and-destroy game with squirt guns as weapons. The targets are pages or pieces of pages from paint-with-water coloring books attached to players' backs. After the battle, the defeated platoon is the one with the most hits—and the hits will be obvious. You can make the game as elaborate or as simple as you want with the following modifications:

- Play in a darkened room. If you want to indicate players' whereabouts, players can wear a strip of glow-in-the-dark tape. If you want teams identifiable, label players with a few small glow-strips arranged in a team pattern.
- For more accurate scoring, cut the coloring-book pages into quarter-sized circles; then glue, tape, or staple them onto a paper towel and pin the paper towel to the player.

Snow Fight

Two teams are separated by a row of chairs, and each is given a three-foot stack of newspapers. The teams have one minute to wad the paper into balls. When the signal is given, each team attempts to throw the most paper on the other team's side before the time limit. Each round is separated by a 30-second break to find everyone who might be buried in the mountain of paper. There will be such a mess that you can easily declare a tie.

Speed Ball

Have two equal teams of players form concentric circles, both facing out. The players can be seated or standing. Each team is given two different kinds of balls (football, volleyball, playground ball, or plastic ball). The object of the game is to move the balls around each of the circles as fast as possible. The two teams move their balls in opposite directions. Any player dropping one of the balls is out of the game and must leave the circle. At the end of the designated time period, the team with the most players left wins.

Strike Force

If you have a number of kids who make airplanes out of your Sunday school papers, here's a game that puts their expertise to good use! You need a gym or a large room, marked into a court. The leader will need a whistle to signal the teams.

Divide the group into two teams, each having a "home front" (safe zone), with a "battle zone" in the middle. Choose a Referee. Each person makes a paper airplane and a paper wad "grenade." The object of the game is similar to dodgeball, except that planes and gre-

| Team A Home Front | BATTLE ZONE | Team B Home Front |

nades are used to hit opponents. If a player is hit with a plane, she hands over her plane and is out of the game. If a player is hit with a grenade, he forfeits his plane and can throw only grenades. He must also remain in the battle zone at all times and any planes that he picks up must be *handed* to a teammate. Keep several Safety Guards on the alert at all times.

Additional Rules:

1. Airplanes and grenades must be *thrown*. Simply touching your opponent with your airplane or grenade is considered a "self-destruct," and you are out of the game, forfeiting your planes and grenades to your opponents.

2. Players may not cross over into the opponent's home front except during "air raids," which the Referee will grant at certain times. However, players may stand at the line and throw planes and grenades into the

opponent's home front.

3. A hit on the head or face of an opponent while he is standing (not ducking) is a self-destruct and the thrower is out of the game.

4. "Grounder" grenades and airplanes that slide or roll count the same as airborne ones if they touch you. Airplanes and grenades cannot be picked up until they *stop* moving. (They can't be stopped with your foot, either.) Grenades and airplanes that bounce off the wall are dead and don't count as hits.

5. Hand-to-hand combat is not permitted and is sudden death to the player who starts it.

6. Change the rules to suit your safety requirement and group needs.

Signals:

1. One long whistle = both teams retreat to the home front.

2. Two short whistles = air raid.

3. One short whistle = attack—all players must go to the battle zone.

Technicolor Stomp

Here's a great, wild indoor game for which you'll need lots of colored balloons. Divide into teams, assigning each team a color—red, blue, orange, yellow, and so on. You can have as many teams as you have colors. Give teams an equal number of balloons of their color. They blow up all of their balloons and tie them. (Have extra balloons on hand to replace the ones broken during this preparation time.)

When the game begins, the balloons from all the teams are released onto the floor. The object is to stomp on (and pop) all the balloons of the *other* teams, while attempting to protect one's own balloons. After the time limit is up (one to three minutes is sufficient), the popping stops, and each team gathers up its remaining balloons. The team with the most balloons left is the winner.

Tic-Tac-Dart

On a large bulletin board, stick strips of masking tape to form a big tic-tac-toe figure with 18-inch squares. Tape three or four inflated balloons inside each of the nine squares.

Divide your group into two teams, the X's and the O's. A player from the X team throws a single dart, trying to pop a balloon. If he succeeds, the next in line from his team attempts to pop another; if she fails, the O team sends a thrower to the line to try. The catch is this: The team that pops a balloon gets to claim that square with an X or an O. Whichever team gets three in a row wins that round. Keep the Safety Guards alert, since darts are being used.

If you prefer not to use darts, lay out the tic-tac-toe design and balloons on the floor and drop sharpened pencils on the balloons to pop them.

Tube Mania

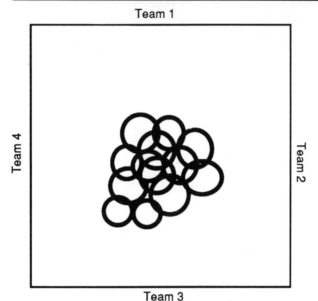

Team 1

Team 4

Team 2

Team 3

Here's a physically exhausting game that can be lots of fun, but might be best if played boys against boys and girls against girls. Mark a large square in the field, and place a stack of seven to ten inner tubes in the center of the square. Divide the group into four equal teams, each one lining up on its side of the square. Number the players on each team from one on up. Place a number of Safety Guards around the playing square.

The object of the game is to get as many inner tubes as possible across your team's line. Call out several numbers. The players with those numbers run to the center and start dragging the inner tubes to their lines. Several players may be tugging on the same tube. Each tube successfully pulled across a team's line scores ten points for that team. Highest scoring team wins.

Water Balloon Whompies

This game is a great way to cool off on a hot day. Nobody wins; it's just fun to do. Team members each get three to five water balloons. Draw a circle on the ground. The entire team sits down inside the circle, while another team lobs water balloons at them. The sitting team cannot move. The throwing team must stay behind a given line, throw the balloons underhanded, and throw on a ten-foot arc. Anybody breaking the rules must sit down on a full water balloon and forfeit play. The teams trade places when one team runs out of balloons. Give a prize to the driest team. You must use the easy-break water balloons for safety reasons. And don't forget to appoint a Safety Guard to monitor the players.

Wacky Sports Events 1

If your group loves sports, but you are concerned that the competition is out of hand, try these traditional sporting events with a twist.

Cup It

Here is a field game that can be played indoors in a large room without carpeting. Break the group into two equal teams. Team A is at bat first and sits behind home plate. Team B is in the field, scattered around the room. Every player receives a paper cup.

A batter from Team A throws a Ping-Pong ball into the field from no lower than shoulder height. Team B players must attempt to catch the ball with a paper cup in as few bounces as possible. Team A receives a point for each time the ball bounces on the floor before being "cupped." (Set a maximum of 15 because of the dribble effect of the ball just before it rolls.) Use a couple of Safety Guards to keep track of the bounces. Each member of the team gets one throw, and then the other team comes to bat. Total the points scored every inning. Play as many innings as time will allow.

Additional rules are as follows:

- Out-of-bounds: A line drawn from left to right through home plate, as well as open doorways. The ball cannot be thrown behind the plate or through doorways. Low-hanging lights and other obstructions may also be considered out-of-bounds.

- Throwing (batting): May be done in any direction, but when the ball is released, the hand must be above the plane of the batter's shoulder. Fielders may not stand directly in front of the batter or hinder the batter in any way.

Fris Ball

Any number of players can play this baseball-like game using a Frisbee in place of a bat and ball. (This eliminates the need for a pitcher.) Each team gets six outs instead of the usual three. The Frisbee must go at least 30 feet on the fly, or it is considered a foul ball. The offensive team doesn't have to wait until the defensive team is ready before sending its "batter" up to the plate. This keeps the normal between-innings slowdown to a minimum.

Inner Tube Baseball

The "batter" picks up the inner tube at home plate and rotates seven times, heaving the tube into the field on the seventh rotation. The batter's team may count out loud as the batter rotates to help him keep track of when to release the tube. Although there are three bases, as in baseball, there is no foul territory, so the inner tube may be released in any direction once seven rotations have been completed. (Because the tube can be launched in any direction, there is no need for a backstop.)

Players are out only when tagged with the inner tube. There are no force or fly outs. Defensive players may tag a base runner by touching the runner with the tube or throwing the tube at the runner (take into account the size of your players when selecting a tube size). Any time the base runner comes in contact with the tube, he is out unless he is on base.

There is one penalty in this game and it is called "jamming." Jamming occurs when a defensive player tries to "cream" a base runner with the tube. Award the offended team with a run and allow the base runner to advance to the closest base. Without this rule some players will attempt to start another game called "Maul Ball."

Newspaper Baseball

This is a fun alternative to baseball that kids who have poor batting averages will love. Instead of a pitcher and a ball, set up two large coffee cans over home plate, and place a rolled-up, taped newspaper across the lids of the cans. Batters get a running start to kick the newspaper "ball." Before beginning play, discuss as a group any modifications to the rules of traditional baseball. Your kids will have fun creating their own new game of baseball. Don't forget to appoint Safety Guards to monitor the new rules.

Plunger Ball

To play this favorite variation of baseball, you need a large, light plastic or rubber ball and an old-fashioned toilet plunger. The game can be played indoors or out.

Divide into two teams. One team is in the field and the other is at bat. The batting team hits by poking at the ball with the rubber end of the plunger. The runner runs to first and all the normal rules of baseball apply.

You can change the rules as you see fit. For example, it's usually best to have four or five bases rather than the customary three; they also need to be closer together. Boundaries can be adjusted and positions in the field can be created spontaneously. It's sometimes fun to play with no boundaries. Players can be put out by being hit below the waist with the ball. You can have five outs per inning rather than the traditional three. Players in the field should be required to stand a minimum distance away from the batter.

Three Ball

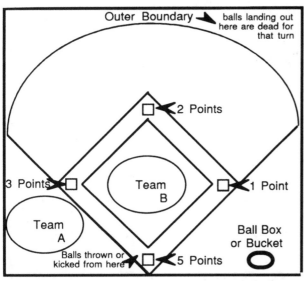

Here's a great outdoor game from New Zealand that can be used with any number of players. You need a baseball diamond (or a reasonable facsimile) and three balls of any kind in any combination. You can use softballs, footballs, rugby balls, soccer balls, volleyballs, Frisbees, or just about anything that can be thrown. You will also need a cardboard box, a trash can, or a bucket.

The box (for the balls) goes near home plate. One team is up and the other team is out in the field, just like regular baseball. There are no positions, however. The fielders just scatter throughout the field. The first batter comes to the plate and selects three balls (if there are more than three to choose from). He must get rid of all three of them as quickly as possible in any way he wants to—kicking, throwing, and so on. The balls must stay within the boundaries of the field.

After getting rid of the balls, he starts running the bases while the team in the field tries to return all three balls back to the box at home plate. The player who is running the bases gets a point for each base he reaches before the balls are back in the box and five points if he gets a home run. If a ball is caught on the fly, then that ball does not have to be placed in the box—it is dead. If the runner is caught between bases when the last of the three balls is placed in the box, then his team receives no points. The runner must watch and stop so that he is safely on a base when all the balls are finally in.

There are no outs. Everyone on the team bats each inning, and the score-keeper totals the points earned. When everybody has batted, then the other team is up and tries to get as many points as possible. You can play as many innings as you want. If you have larger groups, then get several games going at once. It doesn't matter if the fields overlap.

Since it is easy to get to first base (at least), everyone can contribute to the team score and have fun. You will need one Referee to blow the whistle when the balls come in and to help keep score. Boundaries and distances between bases can all be adjusted depending on the size and skill of the group.

Wall Baseball

If you find yourself indoors in need of a game, try this one. It doesn't require typical baseball skills in order to be fun. You'll need a wall (preferably 15 by ten feet, though any size will do), masking tape, a Ping-Pong ball, and a paddle. Use masking tape to lay out a baseball diamond on the floor with a pitcher's mound, home plate, and three bases, as well as to duplicate the diagram on your wall (as seen below) and attach labels. Mark out the bases in front of the wall in such a way that the batter is facing the wall.

Now to play. With her back to the wall, the pitcher tosses the Ping-Pong ball to the batter, who attempts to hit it with the paddle back towards the wall. The play is determined by where the ball hits the wall. If the ball hits in the "double" area, for example, then the batter gets to move to second base. Defensive players position themselves wherever they think they can catch fly balls or prevent hit balls from hitting the game wall. Any ball they successfully prevent from hitting the wall is a strike. All players playing the field must remain on their knees

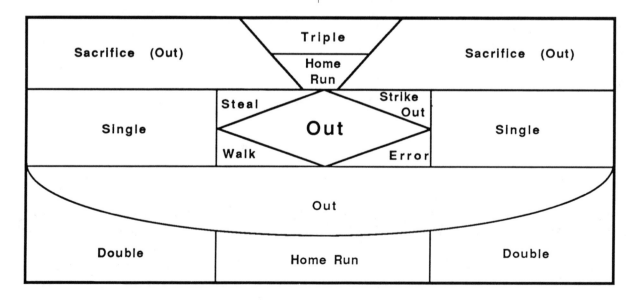

at all times. Balls that hit the floor or ceiling before hitting the wall are ruled as outs. Base runners can do only what the playing wall requires them to do. They can't be tagged or forced out by a player in the field. A defensive player's only role is to block a hit from reaching the playing wall.

A Safety Guard can also umpire, since you will need someone to call obvious strikes and decide where on the wall the ball hit in the case of a dispute. Play as many innings as you want.

Balloon Basketball

Arrange your chairs as shown in the diagram below. There are the same number of people on each of the two teams. One team faces in one direction, and the second team faces the other direction. There can be any number of players on a team, just as long as the teams are equal. The two rows of chairs on each end should face inward.

After all the players are seated, toss a balloon into the center of the players.

Without standing, the players try to "bat" the balloon with their hands, sending it toward the end zone that they are facing. As soon as the balloon drops into the end zone over the heads of the last row of people, the team facing that end zone wins two points. If the balloon goes out-of-bounds, just throw it back into the center. Play to 20 points or for a certain time period.

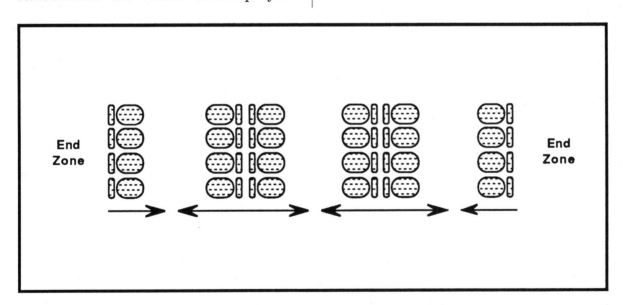

Balloon-Blower Basketball

Have one team line up behind the free-throw line at one end of a basketball court and one team at the other free-throw line. Appoint one Referee and a couple of Safety Guards. Each team designates someone to blow up its balloons. At the signal, the first person in each team's line shoots a basketball from the free-throw line or dribbles as close as he wants to the net and shoots. If that player makes a basket, the "balloon blower" makes one giant blow into that team's balloon. The shooting player retrieves the ball and throws it to the second person in line, who must stay behind the free-throw line until she receives the ball. If the second player makes a basket, the balloon blower blows again, and so on. After a person shoots, he gets back in line. The team that first pops its balloon from blowing it up too big, wins. If you want the game to go longer, give each team two or three balloons. Make sure you keep a number of extra balloons handy. Provide safety goggles for the people blowing up the balloons.

Chair Ball

This exciting version of basketball can be played on any open field or in a large room. Instead of using a regular basketball, use a playground or Nerf ball. You may have any number of people on the two teams. At each end of the playing area, a player stands on a solid chair or wooden box holding a wastebasket or a similar container.

A jump ball starts the game, just as in regular basketball. The players try to move the ball down the field so that someone on the team can shoot a basket. The person on the chair who is holding the basket may try to help by moving the basket to catch the ball when it is shot. All shots must be made behind a ten-foot foul line. The ball may be moved down the field by throwing it to a teammate or by kicking it. You may *not* run or walk with the ball. You may score bas-

kets just like regular basketball, or use any point system your group chooses.

Have a Safety Guard at each end of the playing area.

Fris Basketball

Next time your group wants to play basketball, why not try this one? Instead of a basketball, use a Frisbee and as many players as you wish on a regular basketball court. Of course, you can't dribble a Frisbee, so you must advance it by passing. The Referees should call penalties for fouls, traveling, and out-of-bounds, just as they normally would in a basketball game. Have your Safety Guards double as Referees.

Points are awarded as follows: one point for hitting the backboard, two for hitting the square on the backboard, and three for making a goal (including foul shots). Double the scores for any shot made from behind half-court. Make sure you are in shape before you try this one out!

People Ball

Here's a basketball game that includes everyone, not just the competitive hoopsters. After the group is divided into two teams, five from each team take their places on the court and play regulation basketball—except that they cannot dribble the ball. In fact, they cannot move when they have the ball.

Here's how the ball is moved down the floor: the rest of the team not on the court spreads out along both sidelines, alternating players from Team A with players from Team B. The ten players on the court must throw the ball to a sidelines teammate, who then throws it to a court player on his team. There are plenty of chances for interception, of course, both on the sidelines and the court.

Players should wear identifying colors or jerseys for quick recognition. There are no fouls on sideliners (but Safety Guards need to be watching for any unnecessary roughness), and the ball is always put into play by a sideliner.

Football Frenzy

Choose two teams and divide the playing field in half. Appoint a Safety Guard at each end of the field and also a Safety Guard/Referee. The game starts with each team occupying only its half of the field. Each team gets a football. The object is to complete a pass into the other team's territory within 30 seconds. When the Safety Guard blows a whistle, each ball is hiked to someone on each team to begin play. The Safety Guard/Referee keeps time and blows the whistle when time has expired. After each pass, players must return to their sides of the field.

If the pass is intercepted, the defending team gets six points. If the pass is completed, the passing team gets seven points. If the pass falls incomplete, the defending team gets one point. With both teams trying to complete passes, teams are on offense and defense at the same time.

To make sure jocks don't monopolize the game, make a rule that no one may be quarterback or catch a pass more than once per game, once per quarter, or something similar. Play four five-minute quarters.

Midnight Football

This rowdy game requires special vigilance by your Safety Guards. It is played in a room or hallway that is both free of furniture and other items and that can be made dark or at least dim. If the room is really dark, use a few nursery "night lights" for illumination. The two teams must be even, and you'll need a chalkboard eraser.

First, in the now-dim room, both teams line up against opposing walls, on their hands and knees and with their shoes off. One team kicks off by sliding the eraser over to the other team. A few moments are allowed for the receiving team to make any hand-offs they want, and then play is begun: The receiving team attempts to score by crossing the room with the eraser and touching it to the opposite wall. The kickoff team, meanwhile, swarms out to meet the offense players and attempts to stop their scoring—and this means searching the opposing team's hands.

Teams are permitted to pass the eraser, but they need to be sneaky, or else they'll lose it to the other team. The eraser must be carried by hand across the room. No stuffing it inside clothing, for example. Team members must remain on their hands and knees during the entire game.

If there is a fumble or interception (that is, the kicking team manages to capture the eraser), then play is stopped, and the teams line up again at opposing walls. The team that recovered the eraser now becomes the receiving team for another kickoff. It's wild and a lot of fun.

Broom Soccer

Arrange chairs in an oval, open at both ends (see diagram). Two teams of equal size sit on their sides of the oval. Each team's players are numbered, one through whatever (which means that there are two 1s, two 2s, two 3s, and so

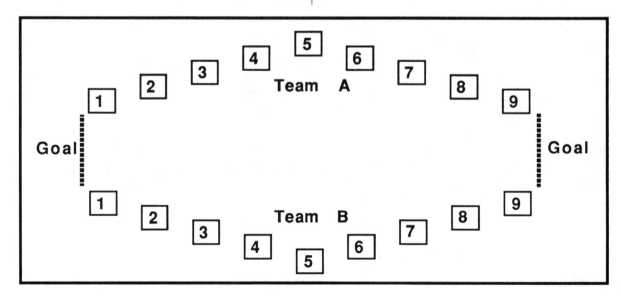

on). Use a plastic or foam ball.

Play begins with a face-off—the two 1s come to the center, each with a broom. After the face-off, they continue playing (since these two are the only ones on the floor), each trying to swat the ball with the brooms through the opponent's goal at one open end of the oval.

The Safety Guard/Referee may at any time shout out a new number—"14!"— and the two 14s must race out to their teammates and replace them. If the ball is knocked outside the oval, it's out-of-bounds—and a Safety Guard returns it into play. Players in the chairs cannot intentionally touch the ball with their hands, but may kick the ball if it is hit at their feet.

Elbow Link Soccer

For a fun twist to the game of soccer, have two teams lock arms with their teammates and face each other about three feet apart in the middle of a playing field. Roll a soccer ball between the elbow-linked chains to begin play. The two chains of players try to move the ball toward their goal at one end of the field and prevent the opposing team from making a goal. The players must keep their chains intact at all times.

Indoor Soccer

With a large, unfurnished room and a six-inch soccer ball, you can stage your own indoor soccer tournament. Adjust the rules to suit your own situation and to keep the game swift and safe. Divide the group into teams of five. In a large group rotate teams in at intervals—two teams play for two minutes before being

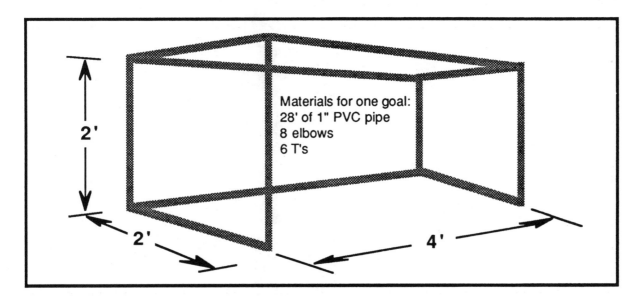

2'

2'

4'

Materials for one goal:
28' of 1" PVC pipe
8 elbows
6 T's

replaced by two new teams. Or keep the players guessing with a tag-team variation: divide a big group into two teams, which subdivide into groups of five. At the whistle (blown at varying intervals), players stop playing where they are, run to their sideline, and tag a new group of teammates to resume play.

You can construct your own goals with just a few lengths of PVC pipe and some inexpensive cargo netting (see diagram). In order to disassemble them easily for storage, don't glue the pipe connections.

Inner Tube Soccer

Using regular soccer rules, substitute a firmly inflated inner tube for the soccer ball. (Have several sizes handy to test the best one for your group.) You'll need a relatively flat, smooth playing surface so the tube can slide when lying flat. It really gives the game a new dimension.

Monkey Soccer

For a fast-action outdoor game, designate a rectangular area of grass as a "monkey-soccer" field, allowing a width of at least three feet per player. Divide the group into two teams, and provide one ball (volleyball size, but lighter and softer).

The team that has possession of the ball attempts to get it across the other team's end of the field. However, the ball must be kept either on the ground or no higher than the height of the average player's knees. Players may propel the ball only by reaching down and slapping it with their hands (clenched fists or otherwise). While in motion the ball may bounce off a player—even off her foot while she's running—but the player may

not intentionally kick the ball or strike it with any part of the body except the hands.

Whenever the ball travels higher than a player's knees, is kicked, or is held, the Safety Guard calls a foul. Play stops while the Safety Guard places the ball on the ground where the foul occurred. The opposing team puts the ball into play. Whenever the ball goes out-of-bounds, it is put into play by the opposing team at the point where it left the field.

Teams may organize themselves in any way they desire to best protect their end of the court. Each team earns one point when its players get the ball over the opposing team's end of the field.

Rainbow Soccer

Play this active game with two teams and 60 balloons (30 each of two colors). Mix the balloons together and place them in the center circle of a regulation basketball court. The two teams line up on the end lines facing each other. One player from each team is the "goalie" and stands at the opposite end of the floor from his team in front of a large container.

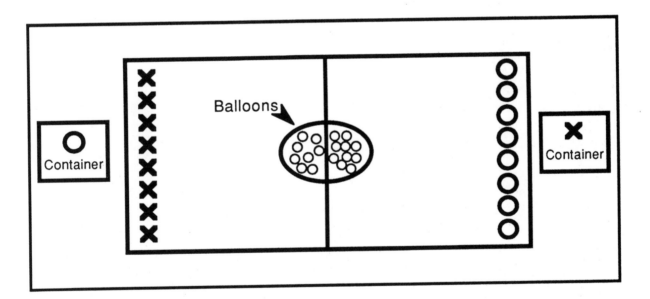

At the whistle, each team tries to kick its balloons to its goalie (using soccer rules), who then puts the balloons into the container behind him. To play defense, a team stomps and pops as many of the other team's balloons as possible. Play continues until all the balloons are scored or popped. If you wish to play more than one round, you'll need more balloons.

Soccerfriz

If you want an active field game that involves any number of players, try this one. Divide your group into three to seven teams of five to 15 players each. Each team should have some kind of identifying mark, such as a colored wristband or cloth. Next, have each team mark a goal (a circle on the ground about three yards across) somewhere on the perimeter of the playing field. Each goal should stand 20 yards from the center of the field and equidistant from the other goals.

The object of the game is for each team to get as many Frisbees (the foam disks work great) as possible into its own goal and to prevent Frisbees from going into other goals. A Safety Guard starts the action by throwing a Frisbee into the group, and the group members take it from there. More Frisbees can be added when the players get the hang of the game. The more the better. Once a Frisbee is in a goal, it's dead and stays there until all of the Frisbees are down, and that round is over.

Here are the rules:

1. Frisbees may be only thrown or rolled. They cannot be carried.
2. Players who have Frisbees in their possession cannot be touched, only guarded.
3. Frisbees may not be grabbed from anyone.
4. If two people catch one at the same time, the call of the Safety Guard is official.

Wacky Sports Events 2

More favorite sporting events with a twist.

Frisbee Bowling

A number of people can play this game that requires very little skill. Several inches back from the edge of a table, set up ten paper cups pyramid-style. From a distance of about 20 feet away, players get three chances to knock as many of the cups as possible onto the floor by hitting them with a Frisbee. Each cup is worth one point. You can call each round a frame as in regular bowling; a game consists of ten frames. To keep the game moving, players can take turns throwing Frisbees, retrieving them, and restacking the paper cups.

Dragon Dodgeball

Have the entire group make a large circle. Send to the center of the circle four or five people, who form a "dragon" by one player connecting with another, hands to waist, until all five are linked.

The players who make up the circle throw the ball at the dragon, trying to hit the last person in the line below the waist.

The dragon moves around the circle,

protecting its "tail." Once hit, the tail moves to the outside circle (becoming a thrower), and the throwers attempt to hit the new person at the end of the dragon until there is only one person left. When that last player is hit, select a new team to dodge the ball within the circle. Allow enough time for everyone to be part of the dragon.

Killer Frisbee

This Frisbee version of basic circle dodgeball has a twist to it that only a Frisbee can add. Form a circle, spacing people so there is enough room to roam in the middle, but not enough so that a player could remain in the center indefinitely. Place half the players in the middle, and let the other half form the circle. With groups of about ten, one Frisbee is enough; larger groups need two or three Frisbees to keep the game moving fast.

The object of the game for those in the middle is to avoid being hit by a Frisbee thrown by players in the circle. Only hits below the shoulders count. If a player in the center is hit, he joins the others in the circle of throwers, and the person hitting that player goes to the middle. Use lightweight or foam Frisbees.

Friendly Four Square

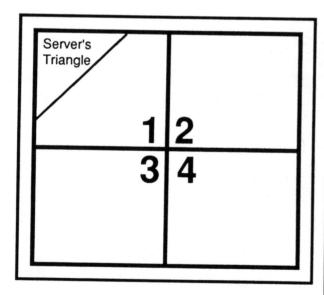

A 16- to 20-foot square is drawn on the floor.

Four players stand in boxes one through four—one player per box. The remaining players line up outside square four. The player in square one is always the server. He hits the ball underhand from the server's triangle (see the diagram) to one of the other squares after first bouncing it once in his own square. The receiver tries to keep the ball in play after it has bounced once in her square by hitting it underhand to a square other than the one from which she received it. Play continues after each serve until someone commits one of the following fouls:

1. Failing to return the ball after it bounces once
2. Hitting the ball out of the squares
3. Hitting the ball back to the person who hit it
4. Hitting the ball with the fist or down-handed
5. Stepping over the server's line on a serve

6. Playing in someone else's square
7. Allowing the ball to touch the body (other than the hands)
8. Holding the ball.

The person who commits the foul leaves the game to stand at the back of the line by square four. The player at the front of the line enters the game in square four. The players in the other squares move up a square to vacate square four. The object is to get into the server's square and stay as long as possible.

Inner Tube Open

This equalizer can be won by sheer inexperience—so look out, golf pros! You'll need one or two nine-iron golf clubs; a dozen tennis balls (six yellow, six orange); a large blanket, quilt, or tarp; and a large, inflated inner tube.

Mark a line ten to 12 feet away from the front edge of the blanket; players take their strokes from behind this line. Place the inner tube on the far edge of the blanket (see diagram). Players get six strokes to earn points in the following ways:

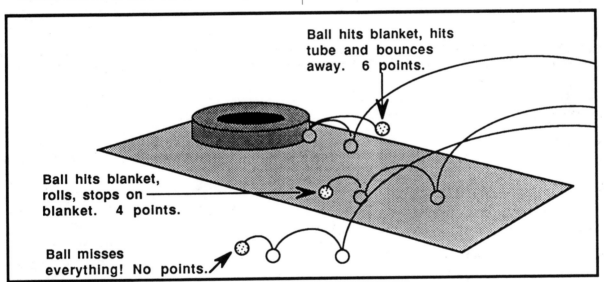

Ball hits blanket, hits tube and bounces away. 6 points.

Ball hits blanket, rolls, stops on blanket. 4 points.

Ball misses everything! No points.

Ball hits blanket	1 point
Ball stays on blanket	3 points
Ball hits inner tube	5 points
Ball stays inside inner tube	20 points

Here's what makes this game fun: Points are awarded cumulatively. For example, if a ball hits the inner tube (five points), rolls across the blanket a way (one point), and remains on the blanket (three points), the player earns nine points. Or if a ball hits the inner tube but bounces away without touching the blanket, that player earns five points. Play with as many teams as you wish. Additional scoring methods:

Ball hits blanket, hits tube, and bounces away	6 points
Missed everything	0 points
Hits blanket, rolls, and stops on blanket	4 points

Tennis Ball Golf

Set up a golf course using various sizes of boxes in a park or other large, open area. Golfers toss a tennis ball, attempting to get it inside the box for each hole. Boxes should be numbered one through nine (or 18). You can make this game as easy or as difficult as you want, depending on the location of the boxes and how the ball can be tossed. You can require that all tosses be underhand, through the legs, over the shoulder, bounced, or however you wish. Usually a player will put the ball into the box only to watch it bounce out. You can also use Frisbees in place of tennis balls.

Hurl Hockey

With one or two dozen plastic gallon milk jugs, you can play a fast court game that's a mix of hockey and jai alai. Cut the bottom out of the jugs in order to make a scoop that can hurl a ball toward a goal (see diagram). Use large boxes for goals. Appoint Safety Guards.

The game itself is played like hockey, though with a whiffle ball instead of a puck. The ball can be scooped off the floor with the plastic scoops and passed to another player or hurled at the goal. Here are other details:
• Start the game with a hockey-type

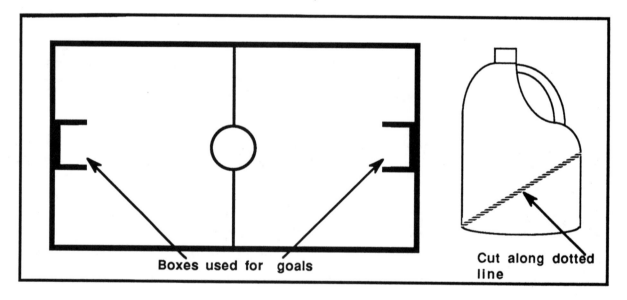

Boxes used for goals

Cut along dotted line

face-off in the center court.
• With the ball in their scoops, players can take only three steps before passing or shooting at the goal.
• The ball can be touched only by the scoop, not by feet or by a player's free hand.
• Traveling (taking more than three steps) or out-of-bounds results in the nearest goalie putting the ball back into play.

Shoe Hockey

This active game should be played inside on a large, smooth floor marked to indicate boundaries, a mid-court line, and goals on each end. (Lines can be marked with masking tape.) Appoint Safety Guards—one at each goal. It's a new version of hockey, played with one soft-soled shoe off and one shoe on. The "one shoe off" becomes the player's hockey stick. A sock stuffed with cloth and tied closed serves as the puck. Each team has five players at a time on the playing field.

The rules are as follows:

1. Each player uses one of his shoes as a hockey stick while wearing the other shoe and both socks.
2. The puck may be stopped by any part of a person's body, but it may be propelled only by a player's hockey stick (shoe).
3. The court is divided in the middle. Three members of each team must remain at their end of the room to guard the goal, while the other two members of each team are restricted to the opposing team's end of the room to try to make a goal.
4. The game is started by lining up five players on one sideline (three from one team and two from the opposing team) to face the other set of five players lined up on the opposite sideline. The lines should be at least ten feet away from the center spot. The Referee places the puck on the center mark, backs away a safe distance, and starts the game.
5. Whenever the puck goes through a goal, even if it was hit by the wrong team, it scores a point for the offensive team.
6. Fouls are called whenever a player hits another player with her shoe, knocks another player's shoe out of his hand, leaves her restricted area, or propels the puck with anything other than the hockey stick. Players may be given two minutes in the penalty box, or the opposing team can simply take a free shot at the goal from mid-court.

Windbag Hockey

A great way to play hockey in a small, confined area is to get teams down on all fours and place a Ping-Pong ball in the center. The teams must then blow the Ping-Pong ball through their goals (a doorway or the legs of a chair) without touching the ball. If the ball touches a player, he goes to the penalty box. Two balls going at once make the game even more exciting.

Crazy Kickball

This game can be played either on a baseball diamond or on an open field. Like regular kickball, one team is up and the other is in the field. The first batter kicks the playground ball as it is rolled to her by a teammate. A miss, a foul, or a ball caught in the air is an out. There are three outs per team per inning. If no outs are made, each player on a team may go up no more than once an inning. When the ball is kicked, the fielding team lines up behind the fielder who retrieves the ball. The ball is passed between the legs of all the players from front to rear. The last team member then takes the ball and tags the runner.

Meanwhile, the kicker does not run around the bases. Instead, the team that is kicking lines up single file behind the kicker, who runs around his team as many times as possible. One run is scored for every complete revolution before the kicker is tagged. Play as many innings as you wish.

Kick the Tire

This is simply a game of kickball using an old, completely pumped-up inner tube instead of a playground ball. The pitcher rolls the tube to home plate for the kicker to kick. It may fly, roll, flop, bounce, or whatever. The kicker can be put out by a fly that is caught or by being hit with the tube en route to the base. You can also use regular baseball rules. Whatever rules you decide to use, this variation of an old game is lots of fun. Don't forget to appoint a Referee to umpire the game.

Kooky Kickball

The group is divided into two teams numbered off consecutively. For every number on one team, there is a corresponding number on the opposite team. The teams line up facing each other—but in opposite order (in other words, the number ones on each team are at opposite ends of the line). A beach ball is used in the game instead of the normal playground ball. The ball is placed in the middle of the floor. When the player's number is called, the players from each team try to kick the ball through or over the opposite team. The opposing team members try to block the ball with their hands but may not kick the ball.

Balloony Ball

Here's an indoor volleyball game that uses a balloon instead of a volleyball. Blow up a round nine- to 12-inch balloon and wrap it up a number of times with masking tape. This will make the ball heavier, faster, and more erratic. Instead of a regular net, use strips of newspaper taped to a taut string that has been run between two chairs.

Players get on their knees to play. The ball can be served anywhere on the court. Your group will want to create other rules; keeping score is optional. The kids will have a great time just making desperate saves and keeping the "ball" in the air. Have a few extra balloons on hand since they will periodically get popped.

Prisoner Volleyball

For this volleyball game, no particular volleyball skill is needed—just catching. Two equal teams take their positions across the net from each other. One team starts by having one of its members call the name of a player on the opposing team, then tossing the ball over. If the other team's named player fails to catch the ball, that player becomes the prisoner of the opposing team and must stand in that team's jail (a designated area away from the court). A Safety Guard is the jailer. A team can get one of its players out of jail by calling out, "Prisoner," and tossing the ball over the net in such a way that the other team drops it. The object for a team is to capture all of the opposing team's members as prisoners. A variation is for prisoners to become members of the opposing team.

Volleyball Water Ball

To play this unique game, you will need a regular volleyball net, lots of balloons filled with water, and two king-size sheets or blankets. There are two teams, one on each side of the net. Each team gets a sheet, and the entire team surrounds the sheet, holding it by the edges. A water balloon is placed in the middle of the serving team's sheet, and the team must lob the balloon over the net using the sheet like a giant catapult. The other team must catch the balloon on its sheet without breaking the balloon and heave it back over the net to the other team. The scoring is the same as in regular volleyball. If the balloon goes out-of-bounds or lands in the team's own court, that team loses a point or the serve. If the receiving team fails to catch the balloon or if it breaks in bounds, then the serving team scores a point. Teams can be any size, but if you get too many people around the sheets, it becomes difficult to move quickly. The game requires great teamwork and is perfect for a hot day.

Wacky Volleyball

This game is played on a regulation volleyball court, with the same rules for scoring and boundaries. The rules for play and the strategy, however, are quite different from the traditional game of volleyball. The following modifications make the game playable for children and adults who are less skilled in the techniques of volleyball—and they provide a new challenge for the volleyball jock.

1. Each team may have four to 12 players. If you have a larger group, rotate players in and out of play.

2. The ball is thrown or passed rather than hit. On each volley, a team is required to pass the ball at least three times before throwing it over. This allows for more involvement by all players. However, no more than five passes are allowed.

3. The ball can be thrown over the net on a serve from anywhere on the court.

4. There is no spiking.

5. A ball hitting the ground counts as one hit.

6. Rotation is encouraged, but not necessary.

The game can be modified even further by using a beach ball instead of a volleyball; by using no net, but a mark on the poles the height of the average player; or by having each team serve every other time. Allow the group to create its own game of volleyball that best meets its skill level and encourages cooperation among all players.

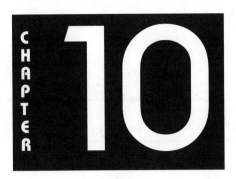

Slow-Gear Games

Slow your group down a bit with these less active, yet still fun, games.

Give everybody a piece of paper and a pencil. Have every person write a name (everyone uses the same name) at the top of a sheet of paper, each letter heading up a column, like the diagram on page 84.

The leader now calls, "Animal," and players write the names of as many animals as they can that begin with the letter heading each column. After two minutes of writing, the leader makes a master list using the animals that individual players have listed. Players receive points for each animal they have listed on their own sheet, plus bonus points for each animal they added that was unique to the list.

This game can also be played with Bible characters, vegetables, cities, or any other category.

This is a great game to play at a social or special event. Before the event write a description of it, using a number of descriptive adjectives. After you have

ANIMAL RUMMY

M	O	R	T	O	N

written the description, go back and erase the adjectives, replacing them with blanks. As guests arrive, fill in the blanks by asking each guest to name an adjective.

When you have completed the blanks, you can then read the description of the event to the group. The results are always hilarious. For example, you may be having a group birthday party. The filled-in blank description could read something like this.

The *outrageous* middle school group of First Church has planned a *stupendous* special event. This *ugly, unbelievable* event has been planned to celebrate the *laughable* group's first birthday. The party is being held at the *marvelous* home of the *yellow* Ms. Collins.

Lots of *dumb* activities are waiting for those *scummy* kids who attend. Bunches of *bleached* prizes await those people who participate.

A *sore* dinner of *odorous* hamburgers, *confused* beans, and *horrible* chips will be served by the *insane* sponsors.

The highlight of this *foolish, awful* party will be the three-foot, *odd* decorated birthday cake. We are glad you could join our *kooky* and *wacky* group.

ßutton! ßutton! Who Has the ßutton?

You may remember this traditional favorite from your own childhood. It used to be called "Thimble! Thimble! Who has the Thimble?" because kids would borrow their mom's sewing thimble.

Here's how to play. Seat the players in a circle with their hands in front of them, palms together, forming a cup. The player selected as "It" moves around the inside of the circle with a button in his hand. As "It" moves around, he pretends to slip the button into the hands of several different players. In the hands of one of those players, "It" really does drop the button. Once the button has been secretly given away, "It" moves to the center of the circle and calls out, "Button! Button! Who has the button?"

At this point all the players seated in the circle guess who among them has the button. Players can make only one guess at a time. The players must continue to keep their hands extended in front of them with their palms together so as not to give away the holder of the button. The player who correctly guesses the owner of the button becomes the new "It" and gets to pass the button. If you do not have a button, use a coin.

Colossal Tic-Tac-Toe and Super Colossal Tic-Tac-Toe

If your kids like to play Tic-Tac-Toe they will love "Colossal Tic-Tac-Toe" (see page 92). And "Super Colossal Tic-Tac-Toe" is great for advanced players (see page 93). Hand out a copy of one of the playing pages, one photocopied page per two players. Both games are played just like regular Tic-Tac-Toe but *all* the squares are used. The game is also scored the same way, with three diagonal, vertical, or horizontal rows making a player a winner of an individual game. Circle all winning rows to keep track of your winnings. The player with the most diagonal, vertical, and horizontal rows of X's or O's is the overall winner. Decide before play whether or not previously used X's and O's can be used to complete a diagonal, vertical, or horizontal threesome row. If you decide that it is legal to count previously used X's or O's to make a new row a winner, you may want players to use different colored pencils or pens to minimize the confusion in scoring.

Continuous Story

Seat the players in a circle where they can see and hear each other easily. The leader begins the game by saying, "Once upon a time . . ." then throwing a small, safe object like a knotted sock, foam ball, or hat to a player. That player must continue the story where the leader left off, then throw the object to another player, who continues telling the story. Continue telling the story in this manner until everyone has had a chance to speak. For added fun, videotape the story telling and play it back for the group.

Crazy Crosswords

Gather your kids around a table for some paper and pencil fun. Play in groups of two to six players. Hand out a copy of one of the three "Crazy

Crosswords," found on pages 94, 95, and 96. "Crazy Crosswords One" is a 5 x 5 grid, "Crazy Crosswords Two" is a 6 x 6 grid, and "Crazy Crosswords Three" is a 7 x 7 grid. The larger the crazy grid, the longer and more complicated will be the game. Each player gets a turn at calling out a letter of the alphabet. Decide the order of play and begin.

The object of the game is for players to create as many words as possible. Words must be spelled correctly and be found in an available dictionary. Words must be spelled from left to right and top to bottom. As letters are called out, players place them in the crazy crossword square of their choice, one letter per square. Letters are called out until all the crazy squares are filled. All called-out letters must be used. Words can be created horizontally, vertically, and diagonally. Abbreviations, slang, foreign words, or proper names do not count. When a word is contained within another word, only the larger word counts. However, an advanced version of "Crazy Crosswords" allows words to be contained within other words. Examples of scoring for both the regular game and the advanced version are shown. Circle all created words to help with scoring. The highest scoring player is declared the winner. Scoring is as follows:

Crazy Crosswords One:

Two-letter words	=	20 points
Three-letter words	=	30 points
Four-letter words	=	40 points
Five-letter words	=	50 points
Dirty words/curse words	=	minus 100 points

Crazy Crosswords Two:

Two-letter words	=	20 points
Three-letter words	=	30 points
Four-letter words	=	40 points
Five-letter words	=	50 points
Six-letter words	=	60 points
Dirty words/curse words	=	minus 100 points

Crazy Crosswords Three:

Two-letter words	=	20 points
Three-letter words	=	30 points
Four-letter words	=	40 points
Five-letter words	=	50 points
Six-letter words	=	60 points
Seven-letter words	=	70 points
Dirty words/curse words	=	minus 100 points

Forfeit

Here is a fun game that takes all evening. As the young people and adult leaders arrive, give them each an equal number of marbles, buttons, or any other small objects that are all alike (15 to 25 will be enough). Tell each of them that if they say the words "yes" or "no" any time during the evening, they must forfeit one of their marbles or buttons to the person they spoke the forbidden word to. If they say "yes" or "no" to the group as a whole, the first person in the group who calls out, "Forfeit," gets the object. It is legal to attempt to trick a player into speaking the two forbidden words. At the end of your gathering, give a prize to the person who has collected the most marbles or buttons.

If You Love Me, Honey . . .

This game usually works best if the group is seated in a circle on the floor or in chairs. Someone is chosen to be "It." "It" must go up to someone in the room and say, "If you love me, Honey, smile." The person must reply, "I love you, Honey, but I just can't smile," without smiling. "It" may make faces, act silly, or do anything except touch the other player to make that player laugh. "It" has three chances to make the person smile. If "It" fails she must move to another person. If "It" succeeds in making the person smile, then the person who smiled becomes the new "It." Instead of replying "I love you, Honey, but I just can't smile," you can substitute, "I love you, but your breath smells awful."

A variation is "Poor Kitty," which is played the same way, except "It" approaches someone and says, "Poor Kitty," while petting the person's head. The person must reply, "Meow." The same rules apply as in "If You Love Me, Honey": no touching—except the petting of the head—and only three opportunities to make the person laugh.

Link

To play this circle game, one person says a noun (dog, clothes, video games, shoes). Moving clockwise, each player must say a word related to the noun (dog—German Shepherd, dog food, bone, fleas; clothes—Guess, shirt, mall; video games—Nintendo, video arcade, Pac Man; shoes—Nike, running shoes, dress shoes, thongs). The same word cannot be linked twice to the noun. If someone fails to link a word to the noun or pauses too long, then that person must start the game over again with a new noun. The object of the game is to get around the circle without starting over.

Mimic

Ask all the players to sit or stand in a circle. Instruct each player to choose another player to copy. Players should choose the player they will copy as secretly as possible. Get the process going by asking the group of players to stretch or spin around. Each player should copy the movements of the player she or he picked. As play continues, the different movements of the group will grow closer and closer together until all or nearly all players are mimicking the same movement.

Miniature Pickup

Players are divided into groups of two or three. Each group needs 15 toothpicks. One player in each group bunches 14 of the toothpicks together between both thumbs and index fingers. The player must then let go of the toothpicks, allowing them to fall randomly. A second player, using the remaining toothpick as a tool, attempts to remove each of the toothpicks from the pile.

Players may remove only one toothpick at a time and can move no other toothpick while trying to remove a particular toothpick. When one of the stationary toothpicks moves, the next player in the group tries her luck at removing the remaining toothpicks. Play continues with each player getting a chance or until all the toothpicks have been removed from the pile. The object is for a player to get the longest run of removing one toothpick at a time without moving remaining toothpicks.

Musical Water Glasses

Break the group into two or more teams; each has eight water glasses, three spoons, and a pitcher of water. Five minutes are given for the teams to put the appropriate amounts of water in each of the glasses to form a musical scale and then practice a song using the spoons to tap the glasses. When groups have completed their compositions, have each group perform before the others. All groups should be given first prize for something—best pitch, most original song, best harmony, most likely to make the top ten, and so on. It's best to put the teams in different corners of the room so they can hear what they are practicing.

One Minute to the Wall

Ask the players to line up against one wall (or behind some sort of boundary). Number the players one, two; one, two; one, two; placing a piece of masking tape on the foreheads of all the number twos. You now have two teams. The players have one minute to reach the wall (or boundary) at the other side of the room. On the word "Go!" players begin to move toward their goals. The object of the game is for members of a team to take exactly one minute to reach the wall moving at a consistent speed.

If most of a team's players reach the wall before a minute is up, or if some of a team's players have to slow way down because they feel they will reach the wall too soon, that team loses. Remove all clocks in the room, and ask players to take off their watches. Each player moves independently of his team according to how fast he thinks he must move to get to the wall in exactly one minute.

OOOOH AAAGH

This concert of sounds is fun to play as well as to hear. Ask each of three volunteers from the group to choose a sound and a body language signal to correspond to that sound. For example, shaking of the head could be associated with the sound OOOOH. Or stomping the foot could be the signal for the sound AAAGH. Choose a conductor and practice a concert of the three sounds with the group. The group should follow the conductor who makes the different body language signals. Add signals/sounds as the group masters the originals.

Ruff, Ruff

Kids have been playing variations of this game in classrooms for many years. Choose a player to be the "dog." He sits at the front of the room with his eyes closed, facing toward the wall. The dog's bone, which for years has been a blackboard eraser, is placed on the floor behind the dog. The leader points to someone from the group and says, "Fetch the bone." The person sneaks up to the bone, picks it up, and returns to the group.

If the dog hears the person fetching the bone, he barks ("Bowwow") and turns around, catching the person fetching the bone. The player who is caught must return to the group without the bone. If, however, the dog barks and turns to find no one fetching the bone, he returns to the group, a new dog is chosen, and play resumes. If the bone is successfully snatched without the dog's knowledge, the person who was able to get it becomes the new dog. The group must keep quiet to give the dog a fair chance to hear.

Switch

This is a funny game that can be played in a short time. One player is selected to be "It." He calls out various activities for the players to perform, such as "Scratch your left armpit with your right hand," "Hop on your right foot while rubbing your left elbow with your right hand," or "Touch your right toe with your left hand." The players must keep doing what "It" instructed them to do until "It" gives new instructions.

"It" can speed up or slow down the pace, at which point she calls new actions. At any point "It" can also shout, "Switch!" and all players must reverse what they are doing. For example, the group members may be tickling their left foot with their right hand. When switch is called, they must begin tickling their right foot with their left hand. Periodically choose a new "It" until as many players have been "It" as time permits.

Touch Telephone

This game is based on the old telephone game, but involves touch rather than hearing. No talking is allowed. Divide the group into teams of four to six players each. Each team sits in a line, one member behind the other. The last person on each team is shown the same simple hand-drawn picture of an object, such as a house, a cat, or a Christmas tree. The person who is shown the drawing then uses her fingers to draw an exact copy of it on the back of the person in front of her.

After feeling the picture, that player duplicates what he felt by drawing it on the back of the player in front of him. This continues until it gets to the person at the front of the line, who then must draw what she felt on a piece of paper. The team whose picture most resembles the original wins that round. The results are hilarious.

Twenty Questions

This is a popular game that has been around for years, and kids still love to play it. The player who is "It" thinks of something that is either animal, mineral, or vegetable. "It" tells the group which of these categories she chose. This is the only clue that "It" gives the group. Play begins with the group asking questions of "It" that would help identify the name of the animal, mineral, or vegetable. The group is allowed to ask only 20 questions to guess what animal, mineral, or vegetable the player chose.

Up and Down

This is another quickie game that's fun to do. Have the players stand in a circle with the leader in the middle. The leader calls out the names of either things that fly, things that swim, or things that crawl. If the leader calls out the name of a thing that flies, the players stand. If she calls out the name of a thing that swims, the players stoop, bending their legs and backs slightly. If she calls out the name of a thing that crawls, the players must sit down. Examples are as follows:

Things That Fly	*Things That Swim*	*Things That Crawl*
Crows	Sharks	Snakes
Bats	Dolphins	Caterpillars
Eagles	Sea horses	Rats
Butterflies	Whales	Snails
Robins	Guppies	Earthworms
Condors	Octopuses	Centipedes
Sparrows	Squids	Beetles
Owls	Seals	Ants
Hummingbirds	Tuna	Ladybugs
Wrens	Bass	Cockroaches
Hawks	Barracuda	Mice
Falcons	Salmon	Gophers
Ravens	Trout	Spiders
Vultures	Tadpoles	Lizards
Flies	Fish	Salamanders

COLOSSAL TIC-TAC-TOE

Directions: Play and score like you would a regular game, but use all the squares. Circle all your winning rows. The player with the most rows with at least three marks wins. (Rows can be horizontal, vertical, or diagonal.)

SUPER COLOSSAL TIC-TAC-TOE

Directions: Play and score like you would a regular game but use all the squares. Circle all your winning rows. The player with the most rows with at least three marks wins. (Rows can be horizontal, vertical, or diagonal.)

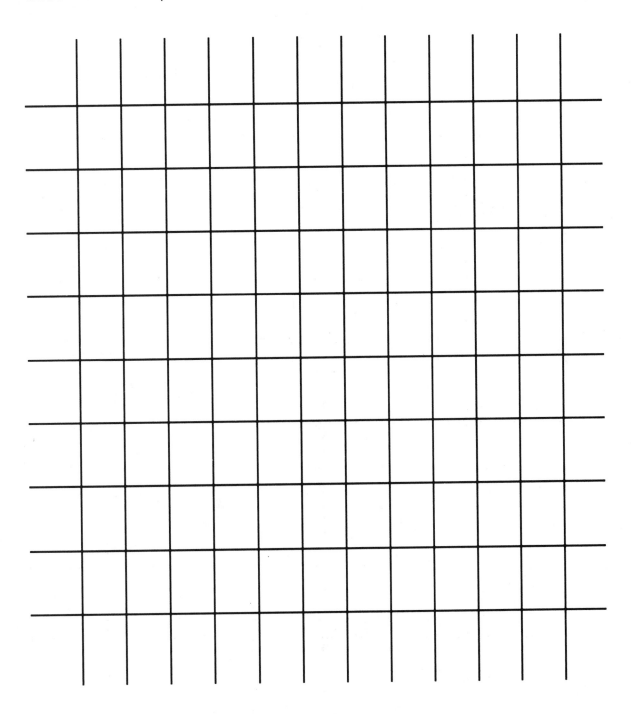

CRAZY CROSSWORDS ONE

Directions: Players rotate calling out letters of the alphabet. See how many words you can create with the letters that are called out. Only one letter can be used in each of the crazy squares. Letters are called out until all the crazy squares are filled. You must use all called-out letters. Words are to be spelled correctly from top to bottom and left to right. Words can be created horizontally, vertically, and diagonally. Abbreviations, slang, foreign words, or proper names do not count. Circle all your created words to help in scoring.

Scoring is as follows:

Two-letter words	=	20 points
Three-letter words	=	30 points
Four-letter words	=	40 points
Five-letter words	=	50 points
Dirty words/curse words	=	minus 100 points

CRAZY CROSSWORDS TWO

Directions: Players rotate calling out letters of the alphabet. See how many words you can create with the letters that are called out. Only one letter can be used in each of the crazy squares. Letters are called out until all the crazy squares are filled. You must use all called-out letters. Words are to be spelled correctly from top to bottom and left to right. Words can be created horizontally, vertically, and diagonally. Abbreviations, slang, foreign words, or proper names do not count. Circle all your created words to help in scoring.

Scoring is as follows:

Two-letter words	= 20 points
Three-letter words	= 30 points
Four-letter words	= 40 points
Five-letter words	= 50 points
Six-letter words	= 60 points
Dirty words/curse words	= minus 100 points

CRAZY CROSSWORDS THREE

Directions: Players rotate calling out letters of the alphabet. See how many words you can create with the letters that are called out. Only one letter can be used in each of the crazy squares. Letters are called out until all the crazy squares are filled. You must use all called-out letters. Words are to be spelled correctly from top to bottom and left to right. Words can be created horizontally, vertically, and diagonally. Abbreviations, slang, foreign words, or proper names do not count. Circle all your created words to help in scoring.

Scoring is as follows:

Two-letter words   = 20 points
Three-letter words   = 30 points
Four-letter words   = 40 points
Five-letter words   = 50 points
Six-letter words   = 60 points
Seven-letter words   = 70 points
Dirty words/curse words = minus 100 points

CRAZY CROSSWORDS SCORING EXAMPLES

Hi	=	20
Ski	=	30
Skate	=	50
Wall	=	40
Atoms	=	50
Pilot	=	50
Total	**=**	**240**

Ah	=	20
Hi	=	20
Pa	=	20
At	=	20
Ate	=	30
Wall	=	40
Atom	=	40
Atoms	=	50
Skate	=	50
Lot	=	30
All	=	30
Ski	=	30
Pilot	=	50
Total	**=**	**420**

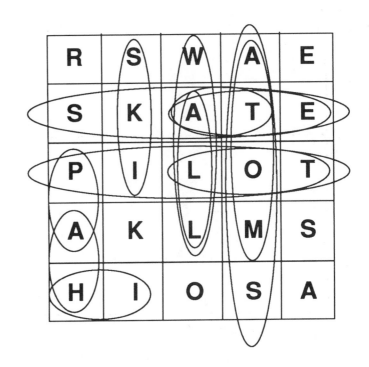